Mapping Patterns of World History

Volume 1: to 1750

Stephen Morillo
Wabash College

NEW YORK   OXFORD
OXFORD UNIVERSITY PRESS

Oxford University Press, Inc., publishes works that further Oxford University's objective of excellence in research, scholarship, and education.

Oxford   New York
Auckland   Cape Town   Dar es Salaam   Hong Kong   Karachi
Kuala Lumpur   Madrid   Melbourne   Mexico City   Nairobi
New Delhi   Shanghai   Taipei   Toronto

With offices in
Argentina   Austria   Brazil   Chile   Czech Republic   France   Greece
Guatemala   Hungary   Italy   Japan   Poland   Portugal   Singapore
South Korea   Switzerland   Thailand   Turkey   Ukraine   Vietnam

For titles covered by Section 112 of the US Higher Education Opportunity Act,
please visit www.oup.com/us/he for the latest information about
pricing and alternate formats.

Published 2012 by Oxford University Press, Inc.
198 Madison Avenue, New York, New York 10016
http://www.oup.com

Oxford is a registered trademark of Oxford University Press

ISBN 978-0-19-985638-1
Printing number: 9 8 7 6 5 4
Printed in the United States of America
on acid-free paper

Table of Contents

Part 4: Interactions Across the Globe

1450-1750

The Global Network

States, Rulers, Cultures

Mapping Patterns of World History

Introduction

There are many ways to tell a story about world history. Textbooks offer narratives, literal stories crafted by a modern historian or team of historians. Collections of primary sources present a mosaic of stories, often interspersed with pictures of artwork and other physical objects, drawn from the past. This sort of mosaic allows readers to take a more active role in constructing an overarching story — they recreate something of the process professional historians use to construct their narratives. Narratives and sourcebooks are often excellent at conveying political, social, and cultural developments in particular societies, partly because almost all sources, written or visual (or even archaeological) come from single societies, with travel narratives forming a rare and valuable exception.

This book takes a different approach to telling a story about world history: it presents the world through a series of maps. Maps are not necessarily a better or worse medium for telling a global story. They are simply a different way, a way with its own advantages and disadvantages. Maps can usually convey much less detail about the political and cultural details of particular societies than narratives and primary sources can. In addition, maps that adopt a "single society" approach — the traditional sort of map of a politically defined country's political boundaries and centers of power — sometimes don't add much. They not only reinforce the sort of "nationalist" perspective narratives can lead to, but can give a false sense of the independence, coherence, and isolation of such entities.

This book attempts to take advantage of the strengths of maps to tell a different sort of story. Maps can reveal connections, by tracing the network connections — of trade, migration, and cultural exchange — and geographic contexts of individual societies. This is valuable because the tension between individual societies, often defined politically, and broader networks, defined economically, socially, and culturally, is arguably one of the central dynamics of world historical development. Maps can also act as snapshots of social history, conveying in dramatic visual terms the aggregate social developments related to demographic and economic growth or change. Like the activities of networks, such deep social trends often do not show up clearly in political narratives or the literary sources generated by social elites. Maps can thus uncover neglected layers of social history. Finally, maps are perhaps the best medium for conveying the trans-regional and even global nature of many such deep processes, from the early emergence of networks of trade through the effect of industrialization on world-wide communications to the impact of global warming on the entire planet.

Such deep processes underlie the organizational scheme of this book. There have been three big eras of human history in terms of patterns of human subsistence and population. The first took off with the emergence in our species of our capacities for symbolic thought, communication, and culture. This propelled our hunting and gathering ancestors across the globe. The invention of agriculture initiated a new wave of population growth and created the agrarian world shown in the second part of the book. Finally, industrialization began reshaping the world once more through impacts still playing themselves out today.

So welcome to a global story through maps — not a replacement for other stories, but a complementary look, another perspective on a story too vast and rich to be told in just one way.

Stephen Morillo
Wabash College

From Human Origins to Early Agicultural Centers

PART ONE

PREHISTORY TO 600 BCE

The early stages of human history are about colonization, migration, and the creation of networks connecting early human communities. These processes began in our modern species, *homo sapiens*, with the emergence of word-and-syntax language and the symbolic culture language facilitated. These linguistic and cultural tools allowed humans to populate virtually every continent, inhabiting a far greater range of climates than earlier hominins had been able to.

The same tools allowed separate communities to trade with each other, and some to settle, develop agriculture, and build more complex societies that traded even more. But not every community settled — some remained mobile by herding domesticated animals and learning to ride horses — and so migrations continued to play a role in emergence and disappearance of early societies.

The maps in this part trace some of the key episodes of these processes.

Maps

▶ 1.1 Colonization of the Globe

▶ 1.2 The Spread of Farming

▶ 1.3 International Trade, 4th-3rd Millennia BCE

▶ 1.4 Empires and Trade, 2nd Millennia BCE

▶ 1.5 Central Asia 2000 BCE-1000 CE and Spread of Indo European Languages

▶ 1.6 Invasions and Migrations, ca. 1200 BCE

▶ 1.7 Colonization and Trade, ca. 750-550 BCE

▶ 1.8 Civilizations: 3000–1700 BCE, 500-200 BCE

Building Early Networks:
Colonization, Migration, and Trade

MAP 1.1 **Colonization of the Globe.** Once homo sapiens began spreading out of Africa, sophisticated technology and adaptable culture made it possible for humans to far exceed the range of earlier ancestors.

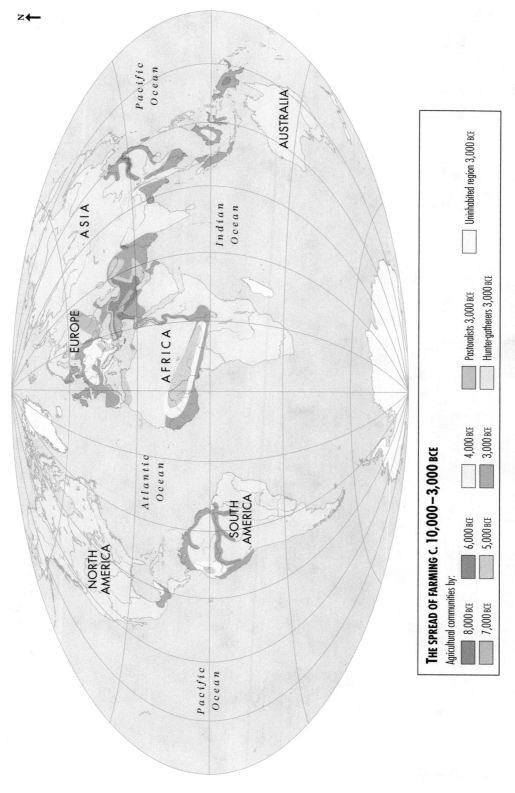

THE SPREAD OF FARMING C. 10,000–3,000 BCE

Agricultural communities by:

8,000 BCE	6,000 BCE	4,000 BCE
7,000 BCE	5,000 BCE	3,000 BCE

Pastoralists 3,000 BCE		Uninhabited region 3,000 BCE
Hunter-gatherers 3,000 BCE		

MAP 1.2 **The Spread of Farming, 10,000–3,000 BCE.** After the revolution of thinking, speaking, and culture that allowed humans to populate the globe, the development of agriculture constituted the second great revolution in our relationship to the natural environment.

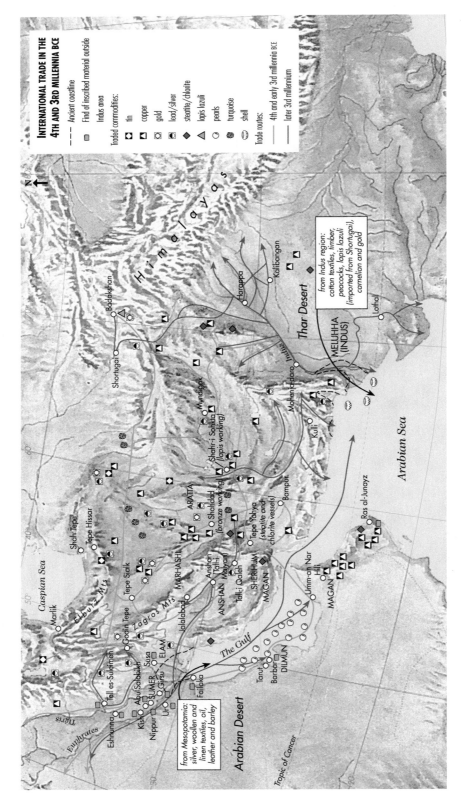

MAP 1.3 International Trade, 4th-3rd millennia BCE. Trade played a central role in the emergence and expansion of many of the earliest centers of "civilizations", or complex, state-level hierarchical societies. Mesopotamia, Egypt, and the Indus River valley civilizations were linked by both land and sea routes.

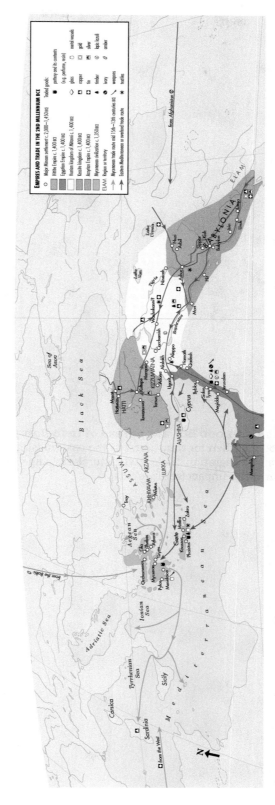

MAP 1.4 **Empires and Trade, 2nd millennia BCE.** Trade not only linked states and empires but contributed to the expansion of complex social organization to new areas.

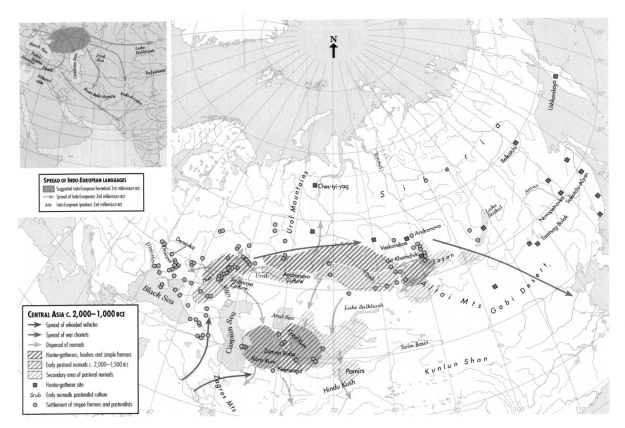

MAP 1.5 **Central Asia 2,000-1,000 BCE and Spread of Indo-European Languages.** The domestication of the horse, first for food and then for transport, put the pastoralist nomads of the Eurasian steppes at the heart of Eurasian systems of migration, trade, and cultural exchange. The spread of the Indo-European languages is one illustration of this impact (see inset map).

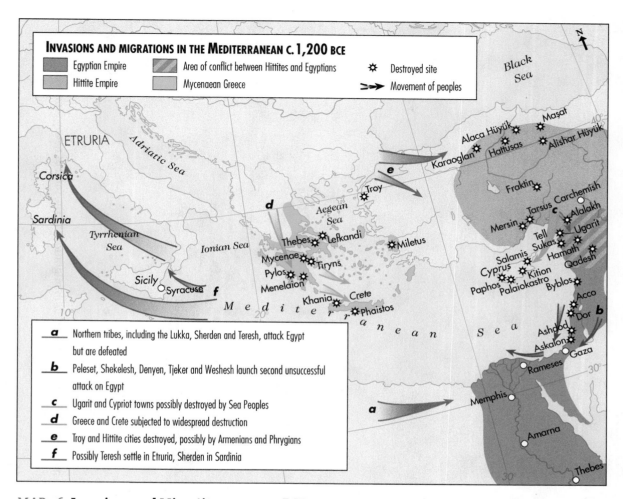

MAP 1.6 **Invasions and Migrations, ca. 1200 BCE**. Migrations that started on the steppes often continued, in a domino effect, far beyond the steppes and even over sea.

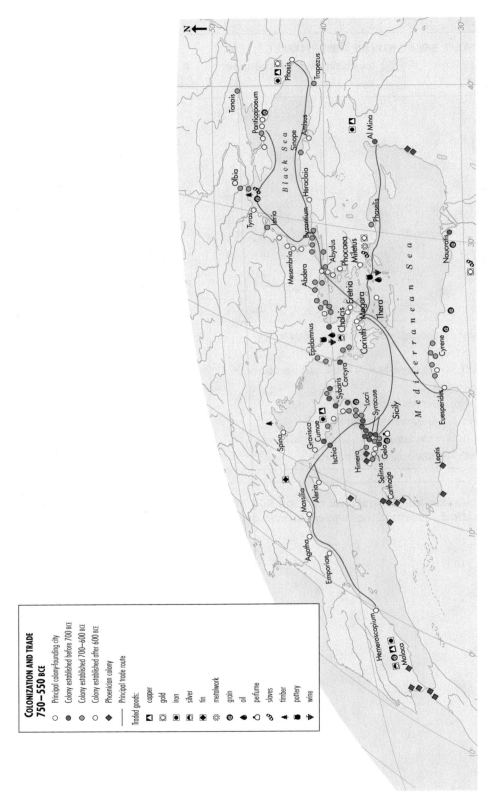

MAP 1.7 **Colonization and Trade, 750–550 BCE.** Trade, especially sea-borne trade, also led to migrations in the form of newly founded.

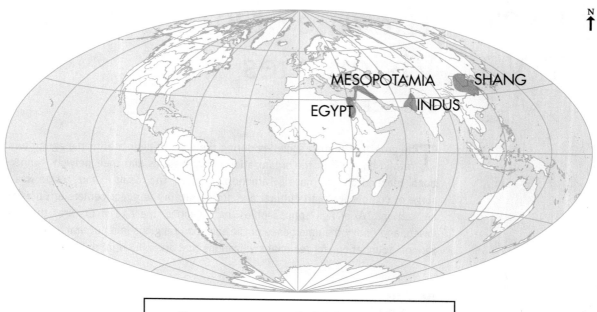

N
↑

CIVILIZATIONS c. 3,000–1,700 BCE

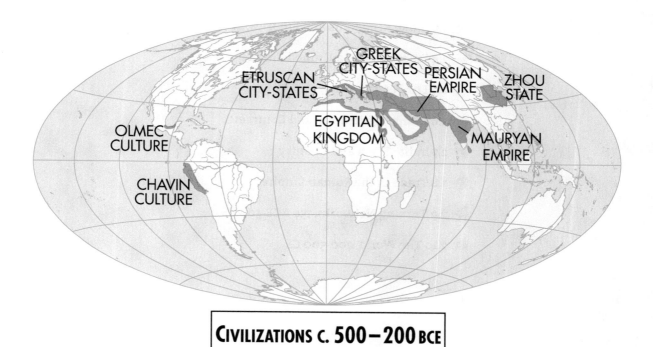

CIVILIZATIONS c. 500–200 BCE

MAP 1.8 **Civilizations: 3,000-1,700 BCE, 500-200 BCE.** In broad overview, the growth of network connections and activity contributed to the spread of complex, state-level societies.

PART TWO

The Age of Empires and Visionaries

600 BCE – 600 CE

The growth of human societies during the early millennia after the agricultural revolution, both in the organization of early states and their network connections, reached critical mass by around 600 BCE. The result in this period was a surge of complexity, both cultural and structural, in the major centers of Eurasian civilization. "Axial Age" philosophies and religions, the Age of Empires that followed, and finally the emergence of the salvation religions laid cultural and organizational foundations for regional civilizations that are influential to this day.

Maps

Axial Age Worlds: World Views and Empires

New developments in philosophy, religion, and political organization appeared in four key regions: southwest Asia, China, India, and Greece

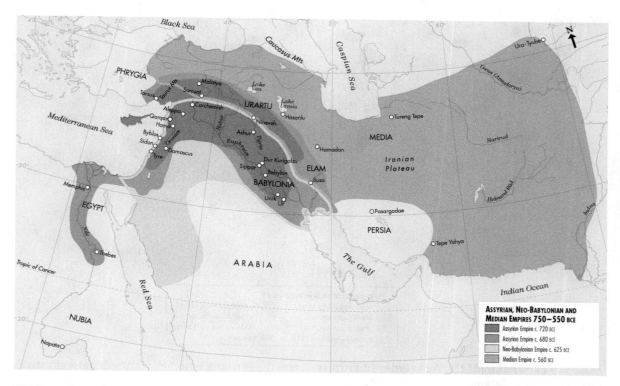

MAP 2.1 **Assyrian, Median Empires.** The Assyrians built the first empire whose efficient administration supported a combined arms military of infantry, cavalry, and siege weapons. But harsh Assyrian rule was undisguised by philosophical or religious justifications and the Assyrians eventually fell to the Neo-Babylonian and Median Empires.

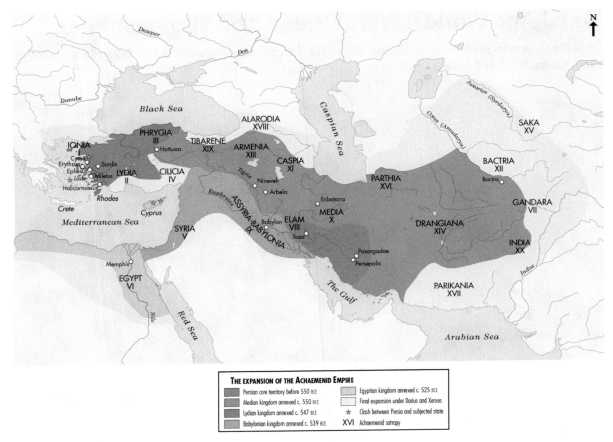

MAP 2.2 **Expansion of the Achaemenid Empire.** It was the Persians, however, who built most effectively on Assyrian foundations by informing state policy with Zoroastrian principles. It was also under the Persians that Judaism developed from early Hebrew religion.

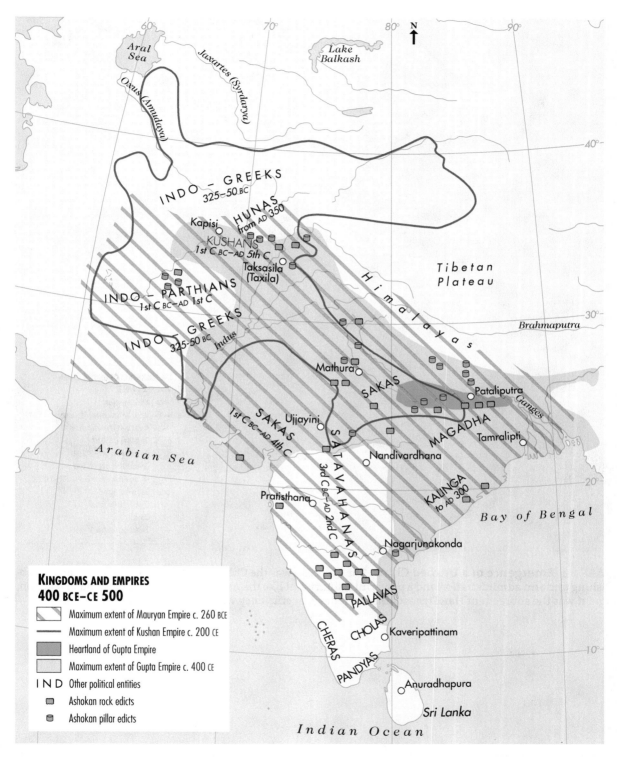

MAP 2.3 **India: Kingdoms and Empires, 400 BCE–500 CE.** The Mauryan Empire created its own combination of efficient administration and benevolent principles when the third Mauryan Emperor, Asoka, converted to and began to promote Buddhism.

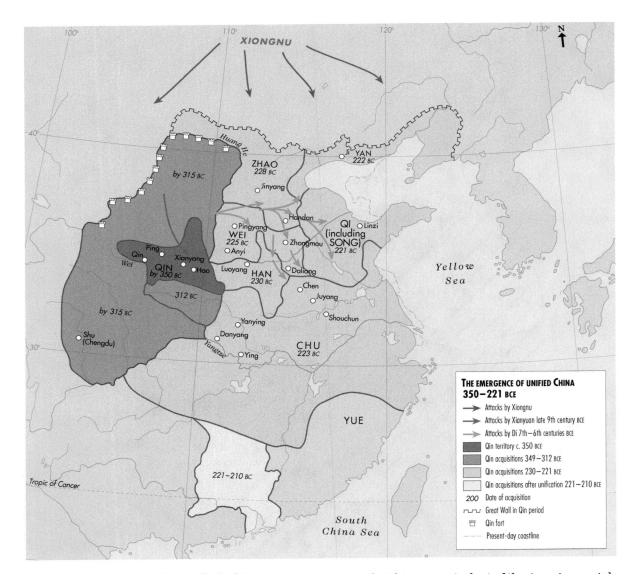

MAP 2.4 **Emergence of a Unified China.** The Qin state was the Chinese equivalent of the Assyrians, establishing uniform administration and a powerful military. But like the Assyrians, their harshness led to reaction, and it was the subsequent Han Dynasty that softened Qin efficiency with Confucian principles.

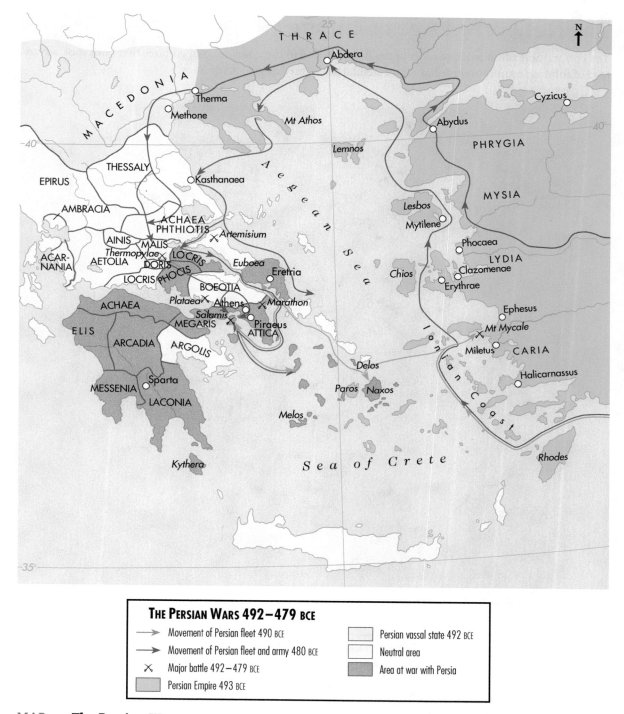

THE PERSIAN WARS 492–479 BCE

→ Movement of Persian fleet 490 BCE

→ Movement of Persian fleet and army 480 BCE

✕ Major battle 492–479 BCE

▢ Persian Empire 493 BCE

▢ Persian vassal state 492 BCE

▢ Neutral area

▢ Area at war with Persia

MAP 2.5 **The Persian Wars.** Persian expansion ran into the fractious realm of Greek city-states from 492 BCE. Victory over the Persians launched the Greeks, led by democratic Athens and monarchical Sparta, into a period of intense cultural creativity.

The Networked Age of Empires

The cultural and administrative tools of the Axial Age led to the flourishing of empires that both took advantage of solid agrarian economic bases and facilitated the further growth of trade.

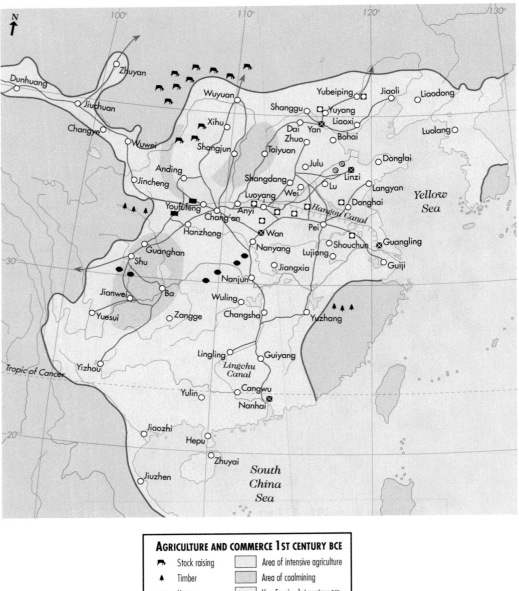

MAP 2.6 **China: Agriculture and Commerce.** Internal communications based on roads and canals were vital to the Han Empire.

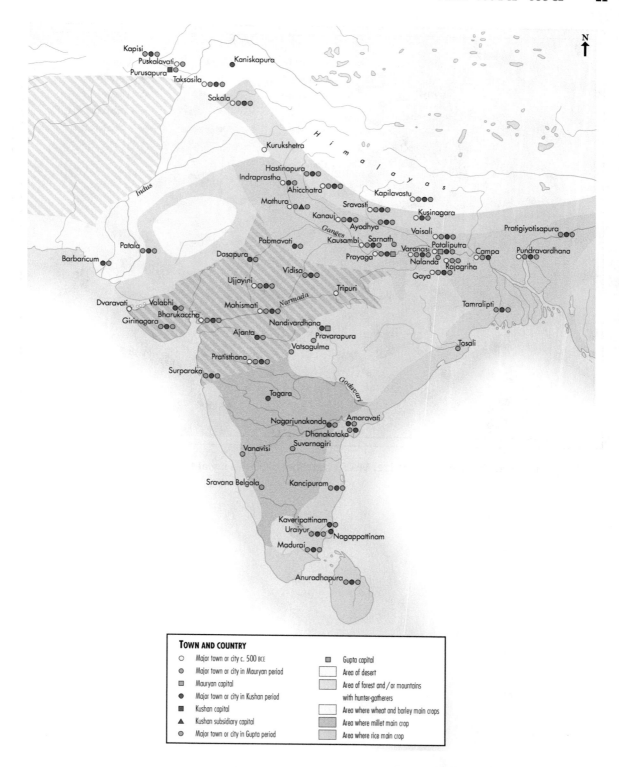

TOWN AND COUNTRY

○ Major town or city c. 500 BCE

◔ Major town or city in Mauryan period

■ Mauryan capital

● Major town or city in Kushan period

■ Kushan capital

▲ Kushan subsidiary capital

● Major town or city in Gupta period

■ Gupta capital

☐ Area of desert

▨ Area of forest and / or mountains with hunter-gatherers

☐ Area where wheat and barley main crops

▨ Area where millet main crop

▨ Area where rice main crop

MAP 2.7 **India: Town and Country.** The relationship between intensive agriculture and urbanization is especially clear in this map of India.

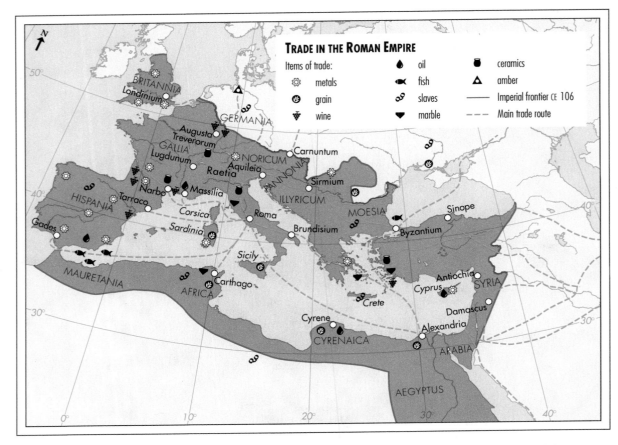

MAP 2.8 **Trade in the Roman Empire.** Mediterranean sea routes lay at the economic heart of the Roman Empire.

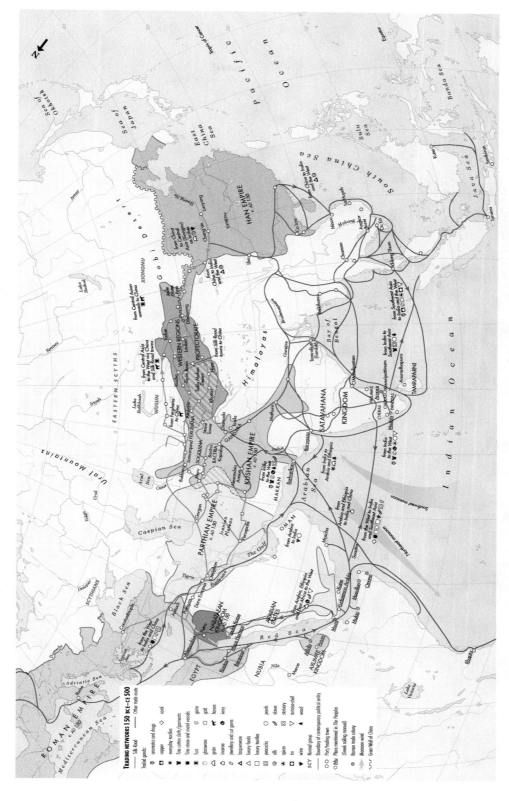

MAP 2.9 **Trading Networks, 150 BCE–500 CE.** The great empires were connected to each other by the "Silk Road" land routes crossing central Asia and the increasingly robust Indian Ocean maritime network, where seasonal monsoon winds facilitated round trips.

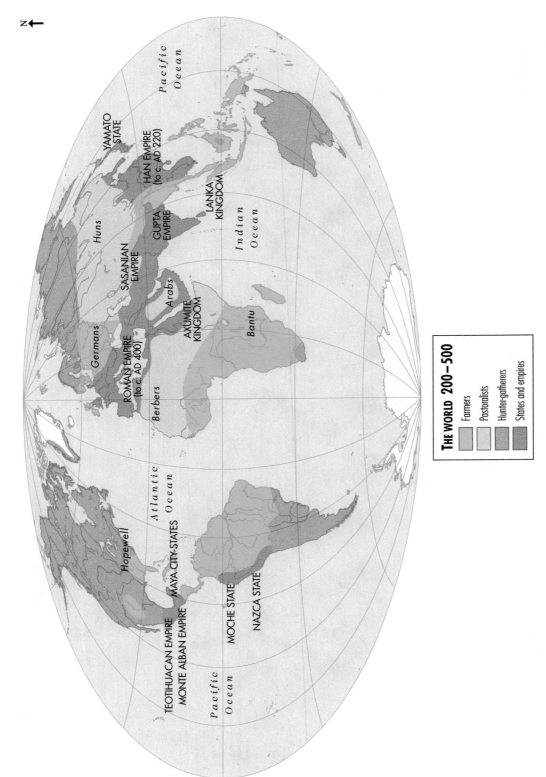

MAP 2.10 **The World, 200–500.** An overview of the world during the Age of Empires demonstrates the connection between agricultural production, trade, and political complexity. State-level societies dominate the temperate zone of Eurasia, while only Mesoamerica and Peru spawned states in more isolated regions.

The Formation of Religious Civilizations

PART THREE

600 CE – 1450 CE

The rise of the salvation religions created large cultural-civilization regions, but development of more localized states and traditions continued in this period. A survey of them could be divided in many ways. Here, the pastoralist nomads of the central Asian steppes played a central role, with the world divided into concentric circuits based on distance from (and connection with) the steppes.

Maps

The Salvation Religions

The emergence of the salvation religions—Mahayana Buddhism, Devotional Hinduism, Christianity, and finally Islam—both cemented and transformed the cultural legacy of the Age of Empires.

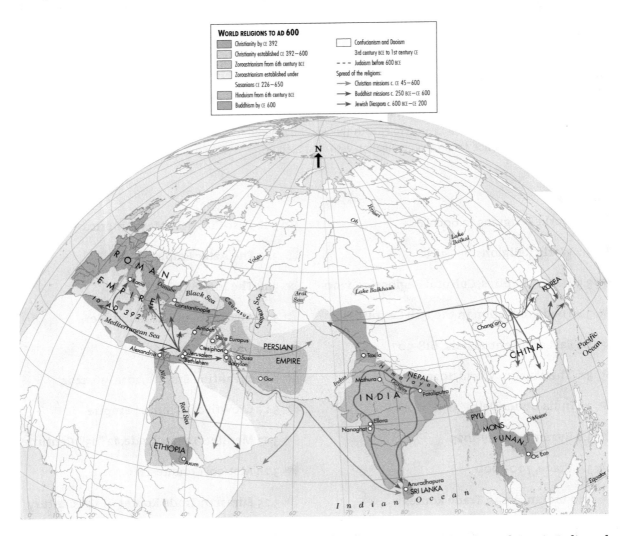

MAP 3.1 **World Religions to 600 CE.** Hinduism, Buddhism (which co-existed with Hinduism in India and with Confucian philosophy in East Asia), Christianity, and Zoroastrianism looked to be established as the major Eurasian religions by around 600.

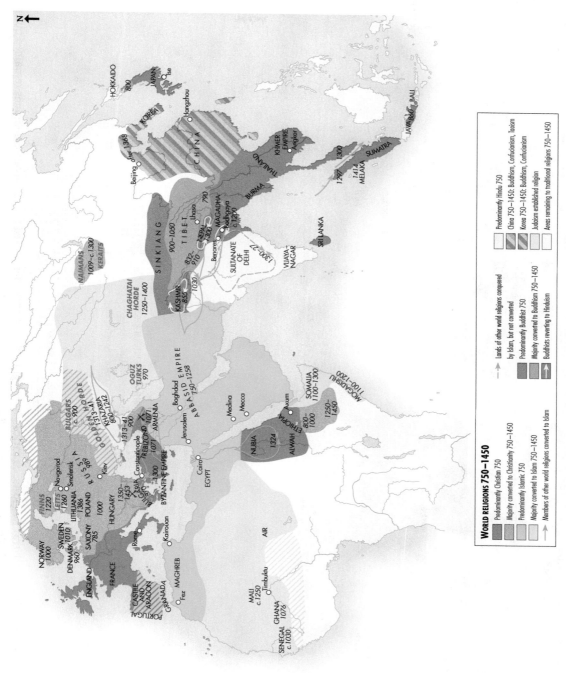

MAP 3.2 **World Religions, 750–1450.** The unexpected and explosive rise and spread of Islam virtually eliminated Zoroastrianism and created a Eurasian religious map directly ancestral to today's.

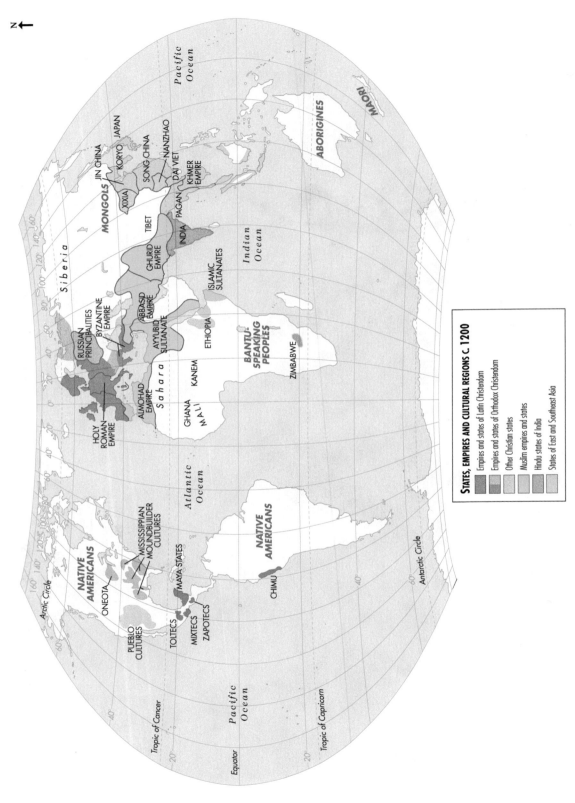

MAP 3.3 **States, Empires, Cultural Regions, ca.1200.** Viewed globally, the areas dominated by the salvation religions remained quite restricted geographically in 1200, but they included the vast majority of the world's population already.

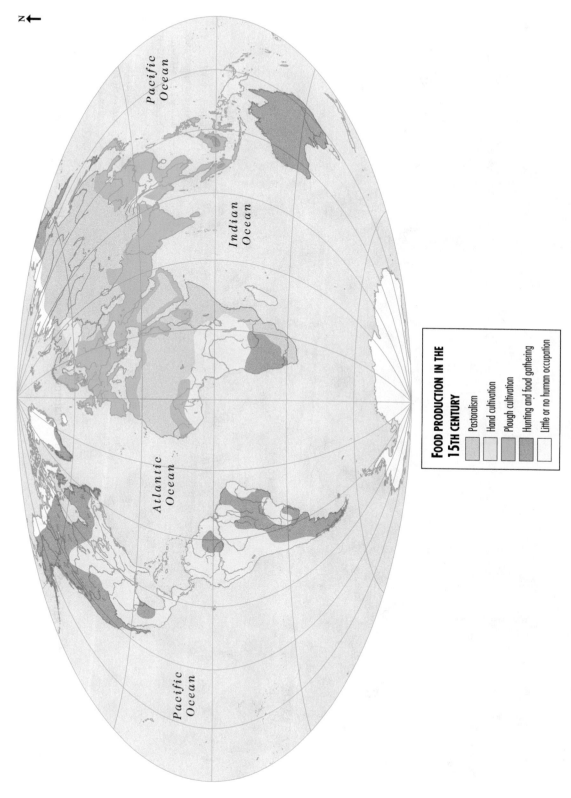

N

Pacific Ocean

Indian Ocean

Atlantic Ocean

Pacific Ocean

FOOD PRODUCTION IN THE 15TH CENTURY

Pastoralism

Hand cultivation

Plough cultivation

Hunting and food gathering

Little or no human occupation

MAP 3.4 **Food Production in the 15th Century.** An overview of food production in the 15th century establishes the basic economic foundations of regional patterns of development.

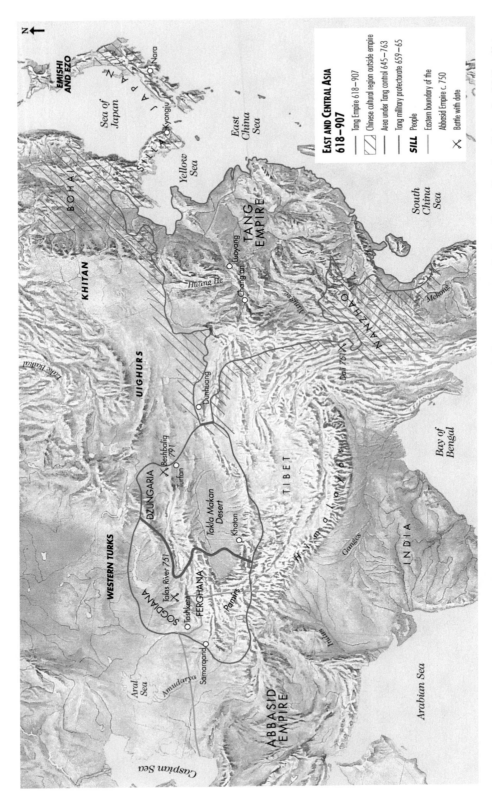

MAP 3.5 **East and Central Asia, 618-907.** Tang China mastered relations with the steppe nomads for a time, allowing it to rebuild the Chinese Empire.

EAST AND CENTRAL ASIA 618–907

— Tang Empire 618–907
▨ Chinese cultural region outside empire
— Area under Tang control 645–763
— Tang military protectorate 659–65
SILL People
— Eastern boundary of the Abbasid Empire c. 750
✕ Battle with date

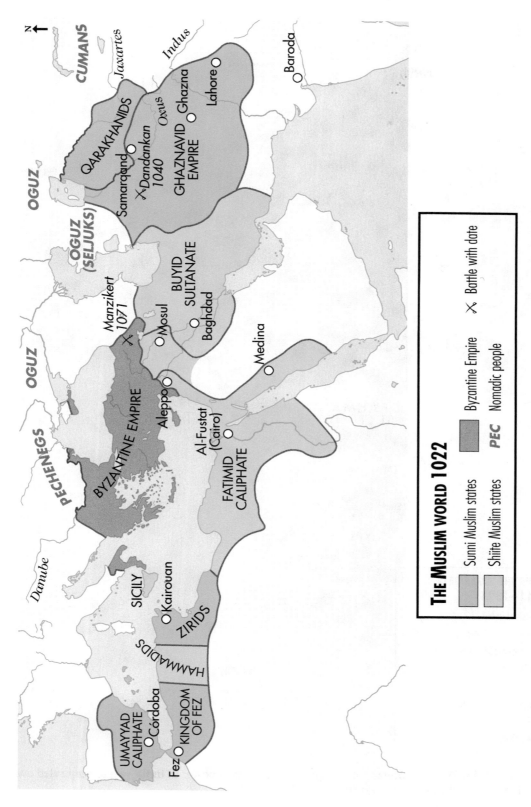

N

CUMANS

Jaxartes

Indus

Baroda

QARAKHANIDS

OGUZ

Samarqand ×Dandankan 1040

Oxus

GHAZNAVID EMPIRE

Ghazna

Lahore

OGUZ (SELJUKS)

BUYID SULTANATE

Baghdad

Mosul

Manzikert 1071

OGUZ

PECHENEGS

BYZANTINE EMPIRE

Aleppo

Al-Fustat (Cairo)

Medina

FATIMID CALIPHATE

Danube

SICILY

Kairouan

ZIRIDS

HAMMADIDS

Córdoba

KINGDOM OF FEZ

UMAYYAD CALIPHATE

Fez

THE MUSLIM WORLD 1022

Sunni Muslim states

Shiite Muslim states

Byzantine Empire

PEC Nomadic people

× Battle with date

MAP 3.6 **The Muslim World, 1022.** The major Muslim states of this period maintained a complicated relationship with the steppes. Many steppe peoples converted to Islam. Some served in the capacity of slave soldiers as the core of the armies of Islamic states. Increasingly, invading Turks became the political masters of Islamic states.

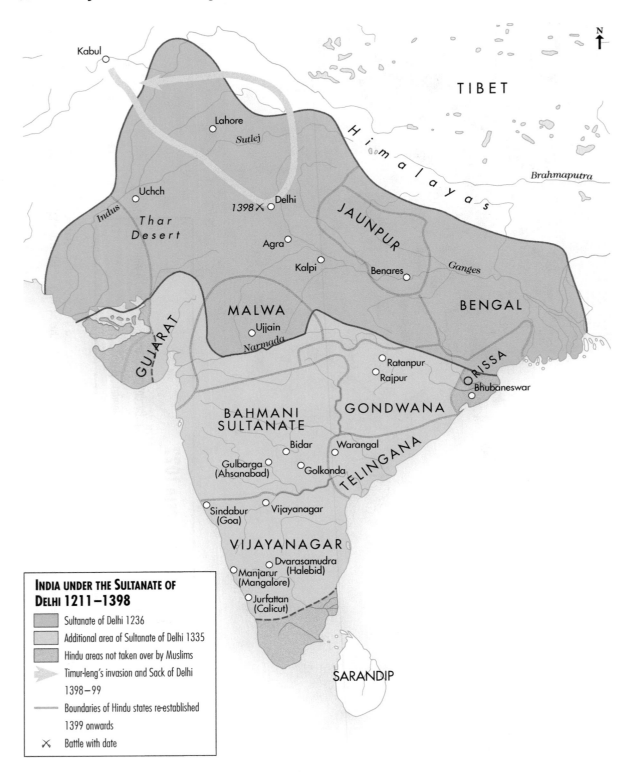

MAP 3.7 **India under Delhi.** Islamized steppe peoples also seized power in India, where they ruled over a population that was Hindu by a vast majority.

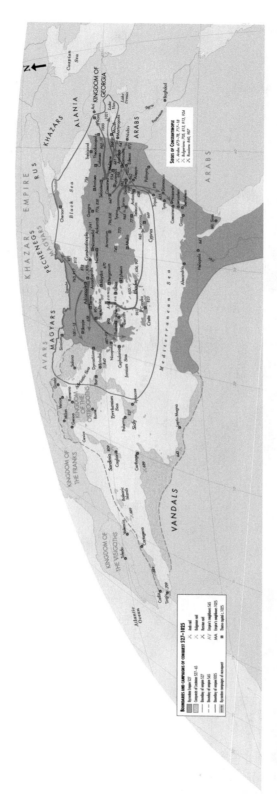

MAP 3.8 **Byzantium, 527–1025.** The East Roman Empire, known more commonly as the Byzantine Empire after the Arab conquests of the mid-600's, maintained diplomatic relations with steppe powers that helped it survive the Islamic assault, but otherwise attempted to keep the nomads at arm's length.

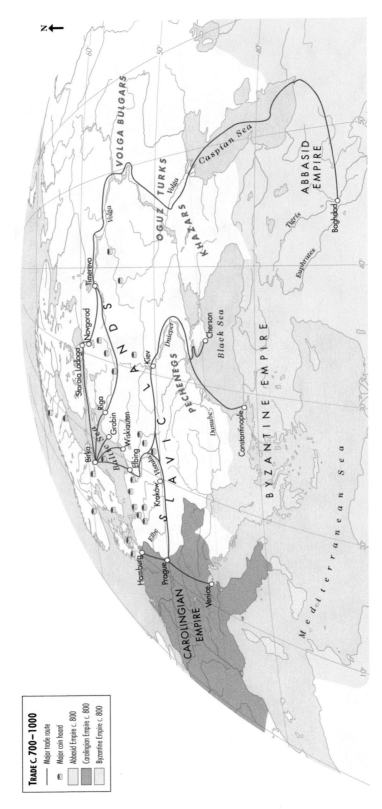

MAP 3.9 **Trade, 700-1000.** In addition to showing the influence of Scandinavian Vikings on patterns of north European trade, this map also demonstrates the marginal position of western Europe in relation to the major Eurasian trade patterns.

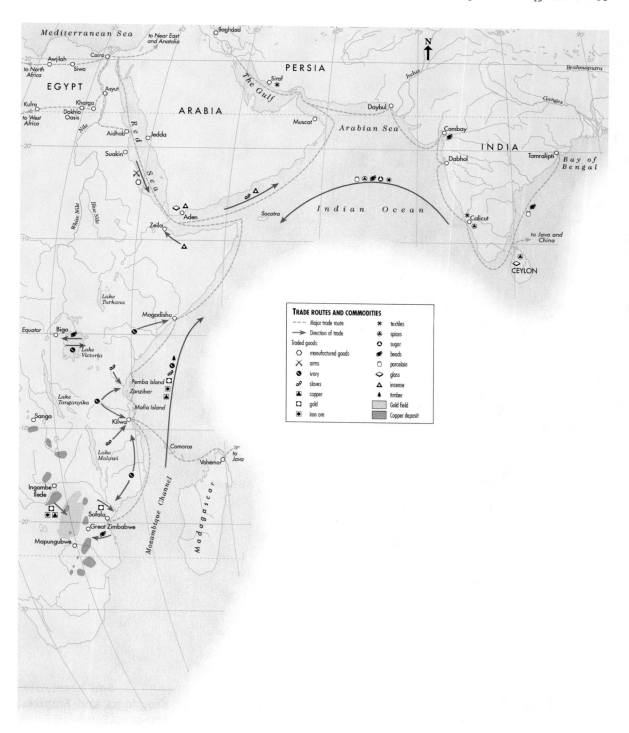

MAP 3.10 **Indian Ocean Trade Routes.** East Africa, like Europe, was connected to major Eurasian trade routes, but in a somewhat marginal way.

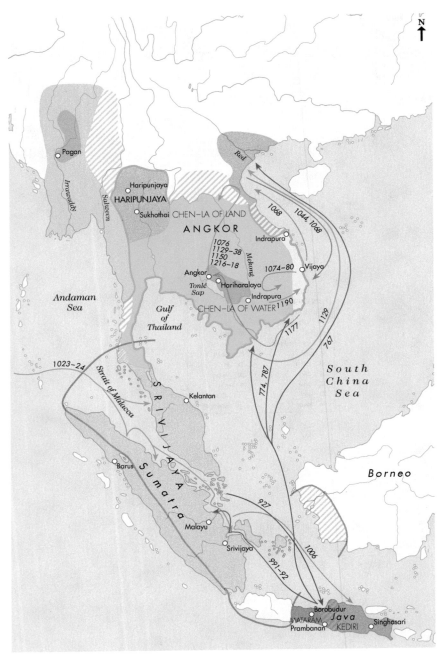

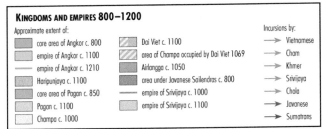

MAP 3.11 **Southeast Asia: Kingdoms and Empires, 800-1200.** Southeast Asia's position along the maritime trade routes between China and India brought it influences from both major centers.

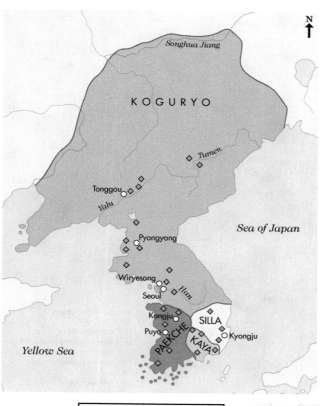

KOREA CA. 600

—— Boundary of kingdom or empire ca. 600

◆ Tomb

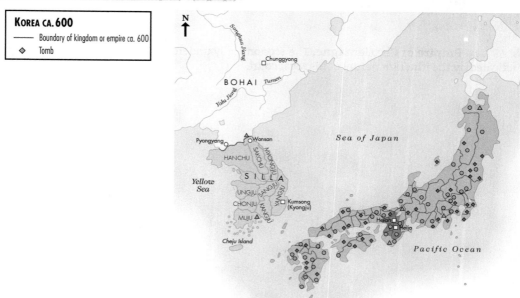

MAP 3.12 **Korea, ca.600, Korea and Japan, 750-900.** Korea and Japan, on the margins of East Asia, were strongly influenced by Tang China.

KOREA AND JAPAN 750–900

——	Boundary of kingdom or empire c. 750	□	Capital
——	Provincial border in Silla c. 750	◆	Buddhist temple
——	Provincial border in Japan c. 800	◉	Shinto shrine
▨	Kinai region	▲	Holy mountain

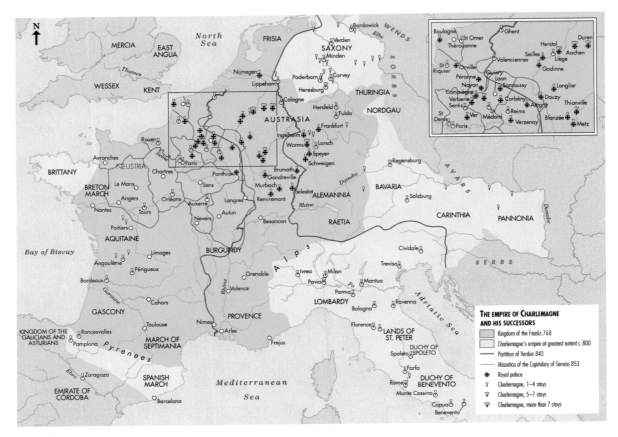

MAP 3.13 **Empire of Charlemagne.** The economically underdeveloped nature of Charlemagne's empire is indicated by the itinerant nature of his royal court.

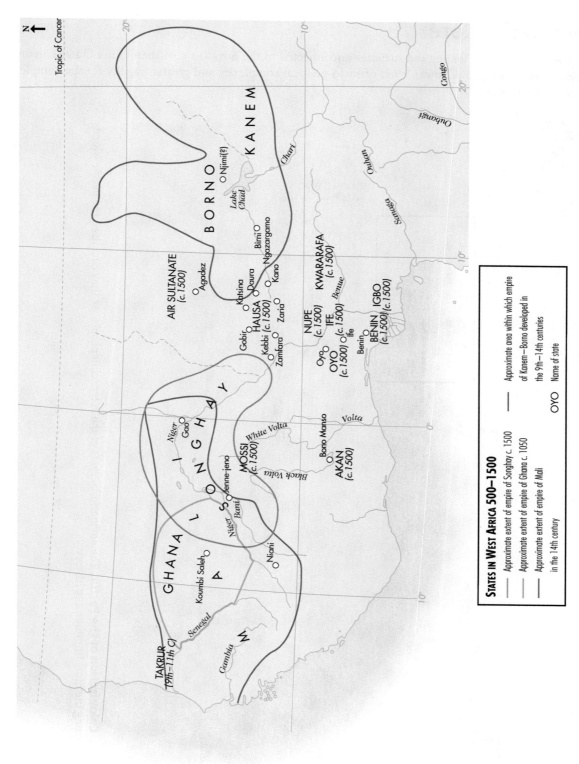

MAP 3.14 **States in West Africa, 500–1500.** A series of West African states were, like other Outer-Circuit regions, connected to the Eurasian Inner-Circuit, but across Saharan caravan routes.

STATES IN WEST AFRICA 500–1500

Approximate extent of empire of Songhay c. 1500

Approximate extent of empire of Ghana c. 1050

Approximate extent of empire of Mali
in the 14th century

Approximate area within which empire
of Kanem–Borno developed in
the 9th–14th centuries

OYO   Name of state

Beyond the Core

Variety was even greater among the societies unconnected to the Eurasian core than in the Outer-Circuit. Isolation often accompanied lower levels of socio-political complexity and greater fragility for the complex societies that did arise.

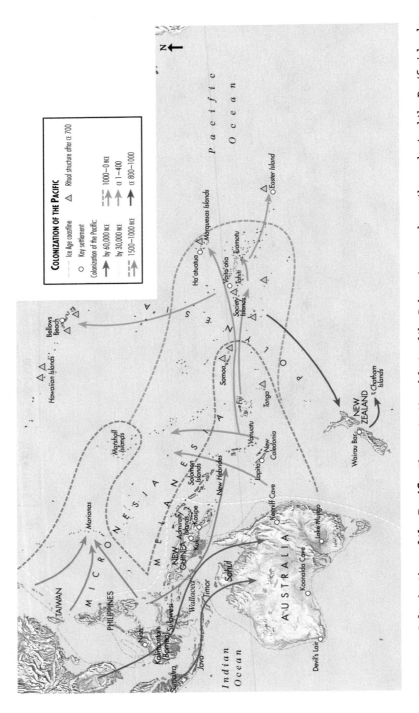

MAP 3.15 **Colonization of the Pacific.** The navigational feats of the Polynesian peoples as they colonized the Pacific islands remain among the most impressive in history.

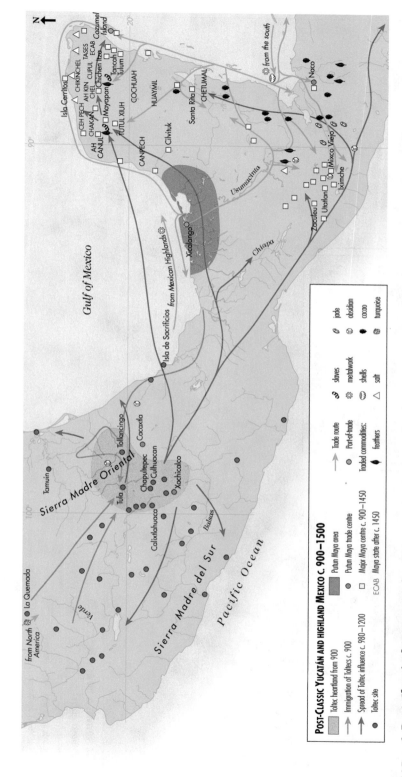

MAP 3.16 **Post-Classical Mesoamerica.** Mesoamerican centers of civilization in the Yucatan and central Mexico were connected to each other, but not extensively beyond that.

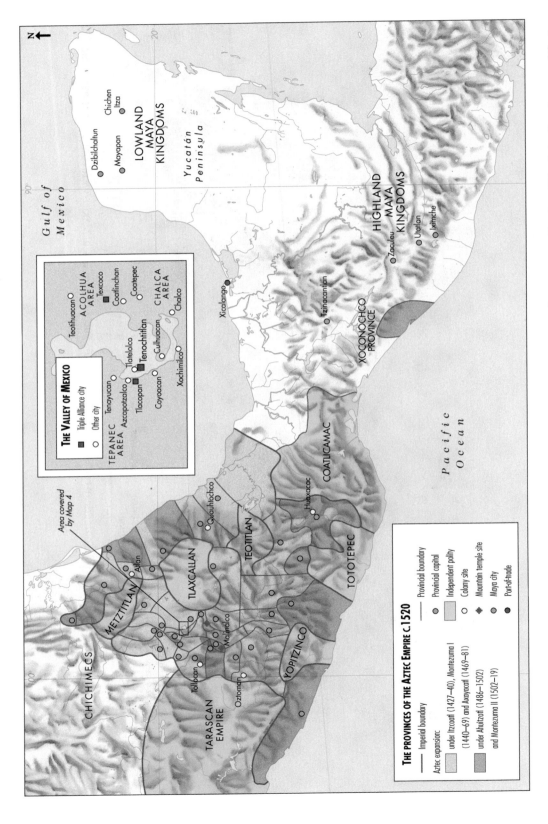

MAP 3.17 **The Aztec Empire.** Though Mayan social complexity regressed after 900, central Mexico saw the rise of the Aztec Empire, one of the two great imperial centers of American societies.

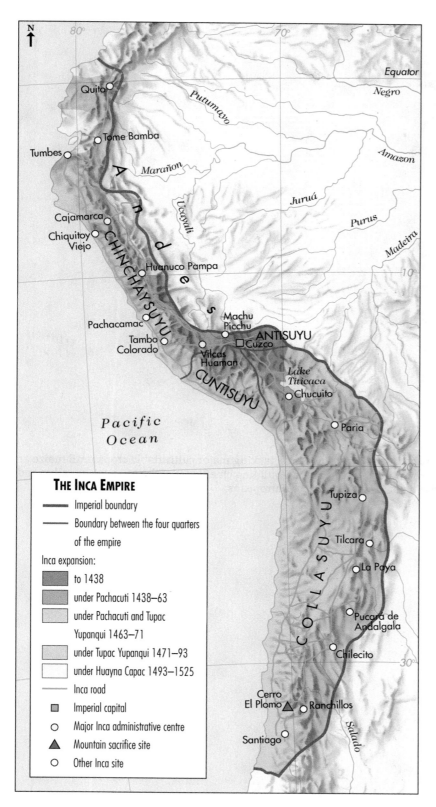

THE INCA EMPIRE

Imperial boundary

Boundary between the four quarters
of the empire

Inca expansion:

to 1438

under Pachacuti 1438–63

under Pachacuti and Tupac
Yupanqui 1463–71

under Tupac Yupanqui 1471–93

under Huayna Capac 1493–1525

Inca road

■ Imperial capital

○ Major Inca administrative centre

▲ Mountain sacrifice site

○ Other Inca site

MAP 3.18 **The Inca Empire.**
The second imperial center
was in the Andes, where the
Incas built an empire that tied
numerous geographic zones
together with an extensive
road system. But the empire
was not networked extensively beyond its own world.

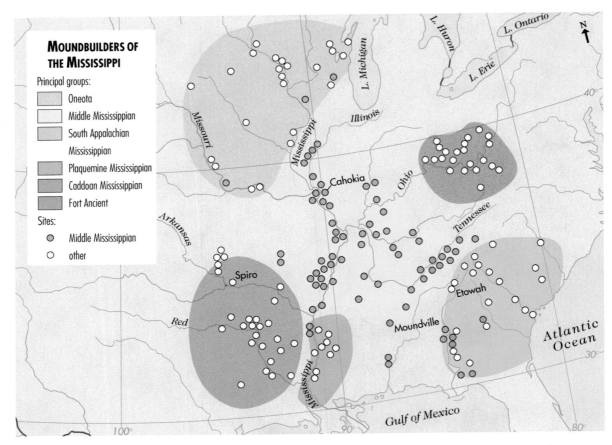

MAP 3.19 **Mississipian Moundbuilders.** North America, lacking major cultivatable crops until maize arrived slowly from Mesoamerica, saw the rise of the mound-building chiefdoms of the Mississippi valley and beyond, but these had dispersed even before the coming of Europeans.

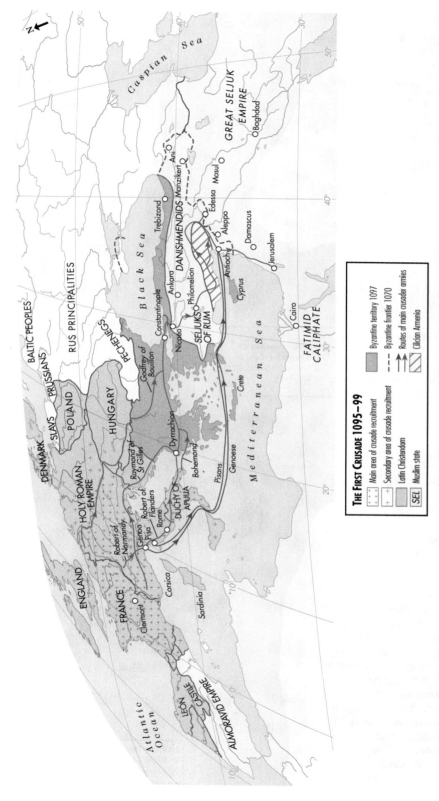

THE FIRST CRUSADE 1095–99

Main area of crusade recruitment	Byzantine territory 1097
Secondary area of crusade recruitment	Byzantine frontier 1070
Latin Christendom	Routes of main crusader armies
SEL Muslim state	Cilician Armenia

MAP 3.20 **The First Crusade.** A sideshow from the perspective of the major Islamic states, the two centuries of European crusading activity in the eastern Mediterranean that started with the First Crusade in 1098 had a significant cultural impact within Europe itself.

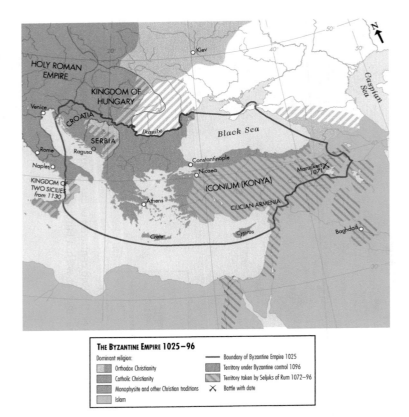

THE BYZANTINE EMPIRE 1025–96

Dominant religion:
- Orthodox Christianity
- Catholic Christianity
- Monophysite and other Christian traditions
- Islam

—— Boundary of Byzantine Empire 1025
Territory under Byzantine control 1096
Territory taken by Seljuks of Rum 1072–96
✕ Battle with date

MAP 3.21 **Byzantine Empire, 1024-96 and 1204.** Of the three major civilizations involved in the Crusading era, the Byzantine Empire lost the most. Their defeat to the Seljuk Turks at Manzikert in 1071, followed by significant loss of territory, indirectly triggered the Crusades. A century of recovery afterwards ended with the sack of Constantinople by western European Crusaders in the Fourth Crusade in 1204.

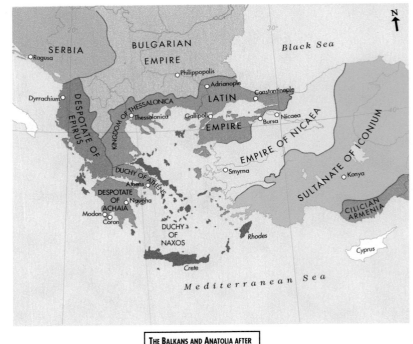

THE BALKANS AND ANATOLIA AFTER THE FALL OF CONSTANTINOPLE 1204
- Latin states

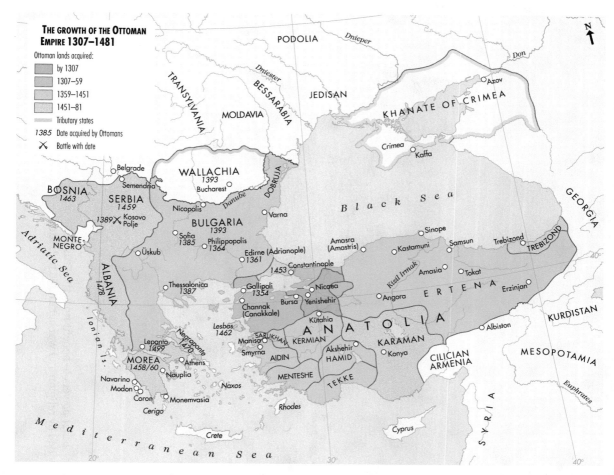

THE GROWTH OF THE OTTOMAN
EMPIRE 1307–1481

Ottoman lands acquired:
- by 1307
- 1307–59
- 1359–1451
- 1451–81
- Tributary states

1385   Date acquired by Ottomans

✕   Battle with date

MAP 3.22 **Growth of Ottoman Empire.** The power that gained the most from the aftermath of the Crusading era was the Ottoman state, which rose steadily through the 14th century.

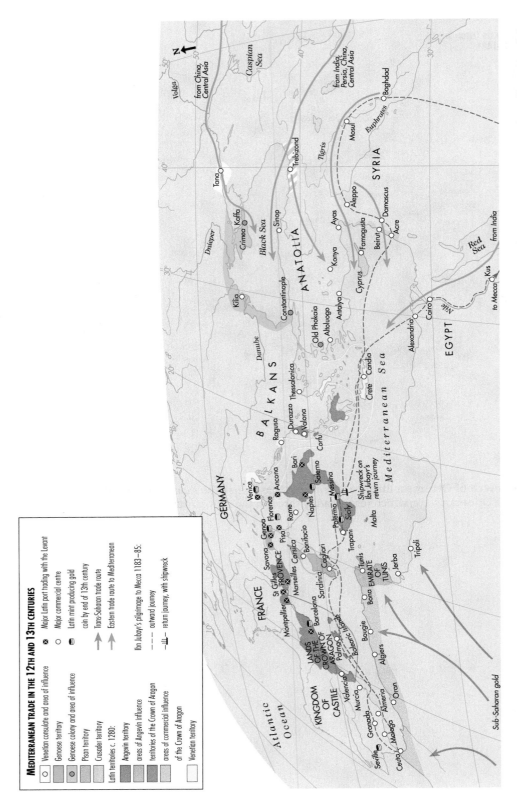

MAP 3.23 **Mediterranean Trade, 12th–13th Centuries.** The other powers to benefit from the Crusading era were mercantile Italian city-states such as Venice and Genoa, as the entire region was not just divided by religion and war but united by trade.

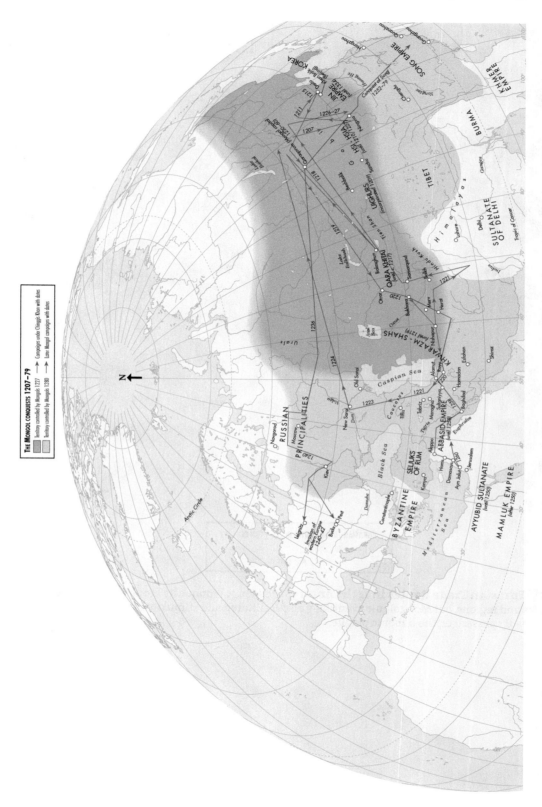

MAP 3.24 **Mongol Conquests.** The thirteenth century saw the explosive emergence of the Mongol Empire under Chinggis Khan and his successors. At its height, the empire united a vast portion of Eurasia.

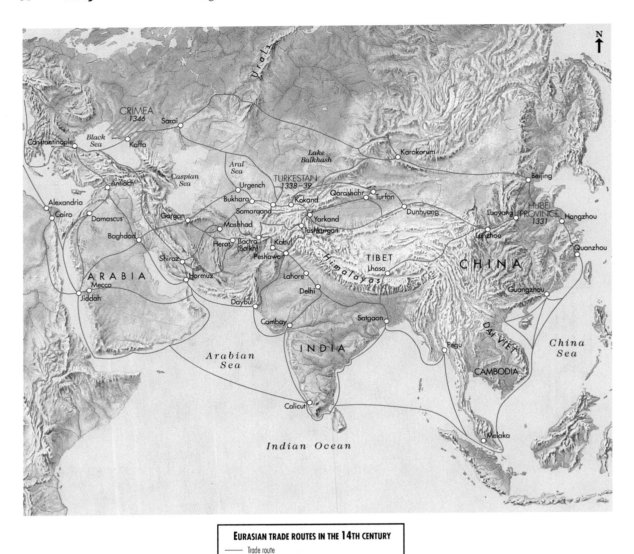

EURASIAN TRADE ROUTES IN THE 14TH CENTURY

——— Trade route

///// Prominent outbreak of plague, with date

MAP 3.25 **Eurasian Trade Routes in 14th Century.** The Mongol conquests brought serious destruction to many cities and regions, but Mongol rule eventually also facilitated and stimulated trade. But the same routes carried a deadly passenger, the bubonic plague.

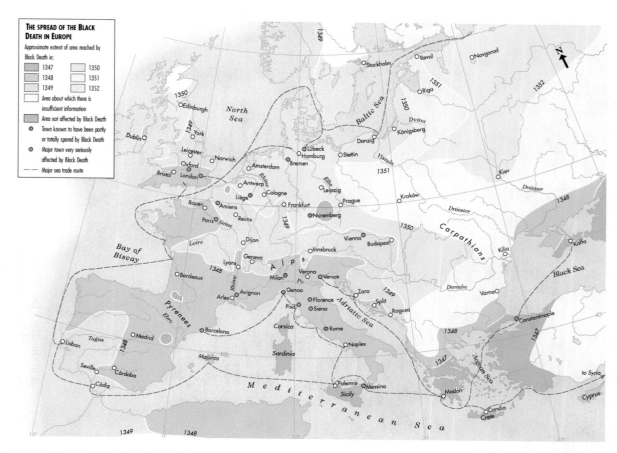

THE SPREAD OF THE BLACK DEATH IN EUROPE

Approximate extent of area reached by Black Death in:

- 1347
- 1348
- 1349
- 1350
- 1351
- 1352
- Area about which there is insufficient information
- Area not affected by Black Death
- Town known to have been partly or totally spared by Black Death
- Major town very seriously affected by Black Death
- Major sea trade route

MAP 3.26 **Spread of the Black Death.** The plague ravaged China, central Asia, and the Islamic world before reaching western Europe, where it killed as much as a third of the population in three years.

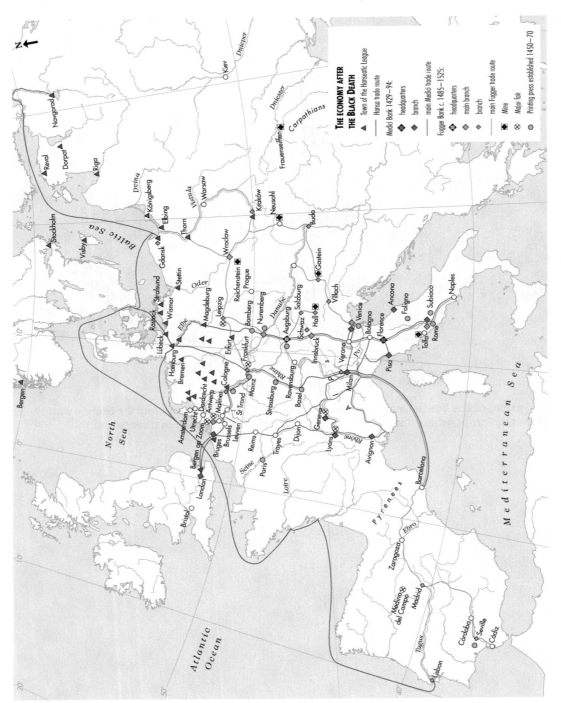

MAP 3.27 **European Economy post Black Death.** One ironic result of the Black Death in Europe was that, by killing people but not destroying property, it left the remaining population richer. Trade and banking grew hand-in-hand as a result.

Interactions Across the Globe

PART FOUR

1450 – 1750

As the regional traditions represented in Part 3 developed and spread, they came into increasing connection with each other through expanding and strengthening network connections. Such contacts ranged from heightened military competition to growing economic exchanges, and always involved cultural encounters. And sometimes they spawned unintended consequences, such as the transmission of the Black Death across the major Eurasian trade routes. By the 1490s, the growth of global network connections began to have serious transformative effects on global patterns of exchange.

The European voyages of exploration, by linking the long-established Eurasian and Indian Ocean trade systems to the peoples and resources of previously isolated regions, especially the Americas, created a truly global network of economic and cultural exchange. The period from 1500 to 1750 then saw the agrarian or pre-industrial world reach new levels of maturity and sophistication economically, politically, and culturally.

Maps

The Global Network

The global network carried flows of goods and peoples (as well as diseases and ideas) that created new systems and reinforced old ones.

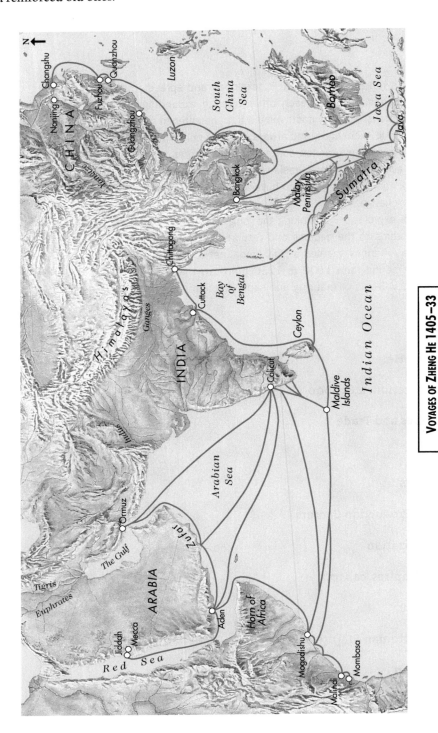

VOYAGES OF ZHENG HE 1405–33
—— Routes of ships from Zheng He's fleet

MAP 4.1 **Voyages of Zheng He.** The voyages of the early Ming Treasure Fleets, led by Admiral Zheng He, asserted Chinese centrality in the vibrant trade circuits of the South China Sea and Indian Ocean.

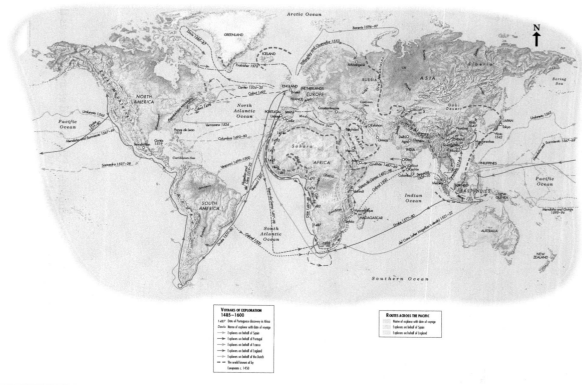

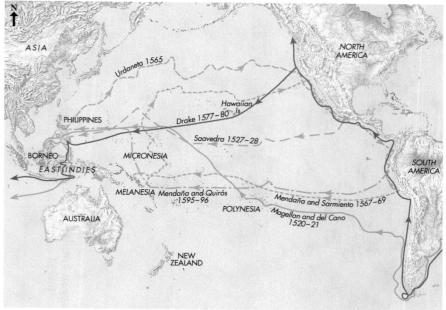

ROUTES ACROSS THE PACIFIC

Drake   Name of explorer with date of voyage

→   Explorers on behalf of Spain

→   Explorers on behalf of England

MAP 4.2 **Voyages of Exploration, 1485-1600.** The most significant expansion of the global network of exchange came with European mastery of the circular wind patterns of the Atlantic and Pacific Oceans.

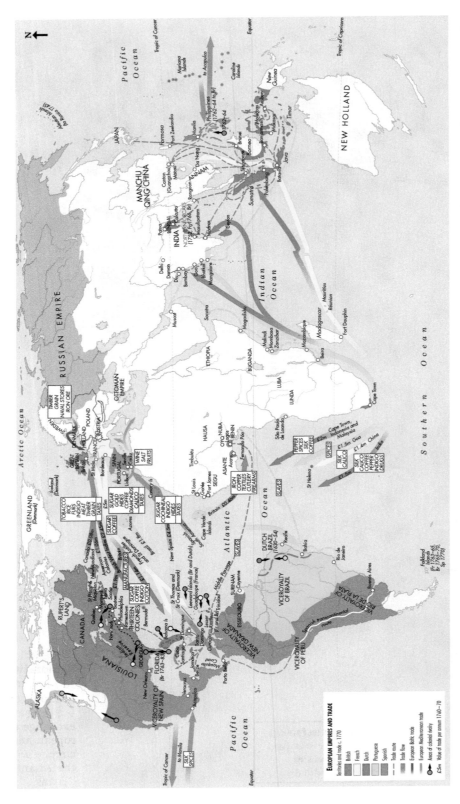

MAP 4.3 **European Empires and Trade.** Although China and India remained the great economic powerhouses of the global economy, it was the new connections forged by European merchants, adventurers, and colonists that reshaped the patterns of global trade.

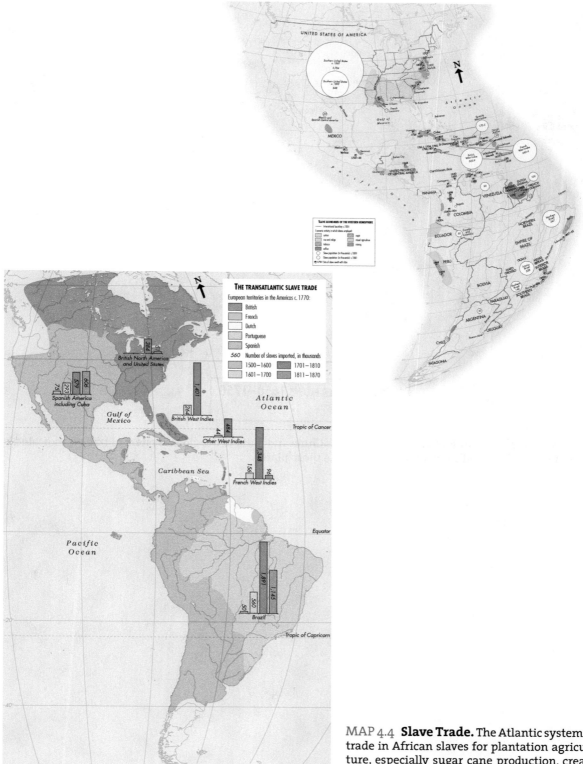

MAP 4.4 **Slave Trade.** The Atlantic system's trade in African slaves for plantation agriculture, especially sugar cane production, created the largest forced migration in history.

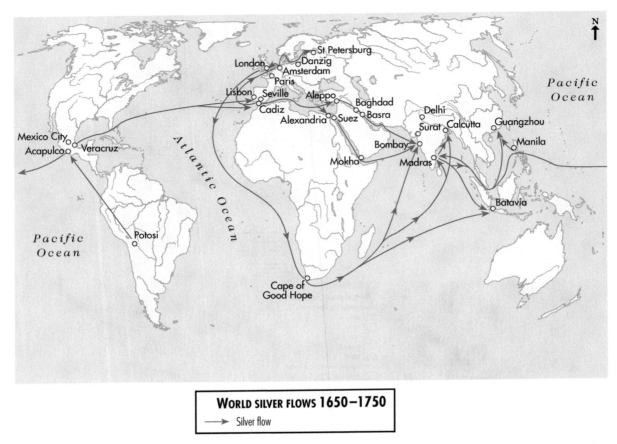

WORLD SILVER FLOWS 1650–1750

→ Silver flow

MAP 4.5 **World Silver Flows.** The centrality of China and India to the global system of trade is indicated by how much of the world's silver flows ended up in those places.

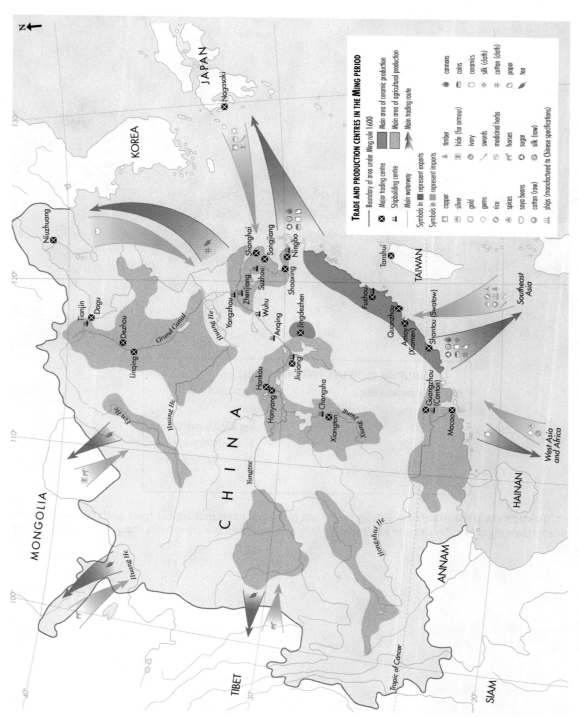

MAP 4.6 **Ming Trade and Production Centers.** The dynamic and varied Chinese economy was strongly connected to the global network despite official Chinese restrictions on the overseas activities of its own merchants.

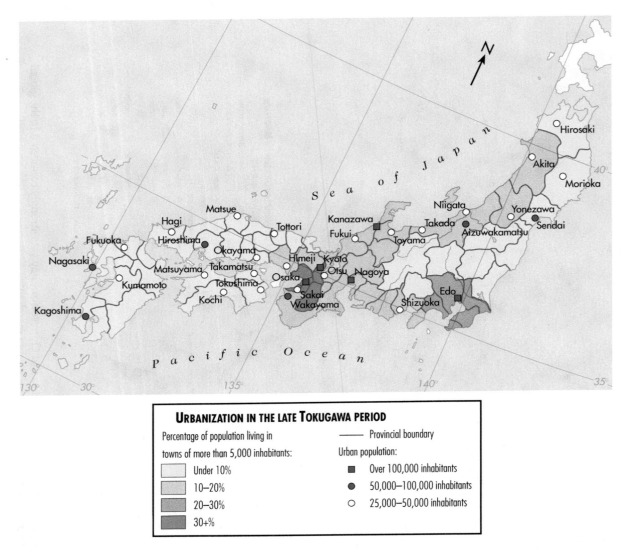

URBANIZATION IN THE LATE TOKUGAWA PERIOD

Percentage of population living in
towns of more than 5,000 inhabitants:

- Under 10%
- 10–20%
- 20–30%
- 30+%

——— Provincial boundary

Urban population:

- ■ Over 100,000 inhabitants
- ● 50,000–100,000 inhabitants
- ○ 25,000–50,000 inhabitants

MAP 4.7 **Tokugawa Urbanization.** Tokugawa Japan provides a fascinating contrast with China. Its internal economy grew significantly despite almost complete, self-imposed isolation from the global network after 1640.

States, Rulers, and Cultures

Against the background of global economic flows, traditional forms of imperial political organization continued to thrive. But the transformative impact of network flows began to affect cultures in various places and to lay the basis for significant political transformations.

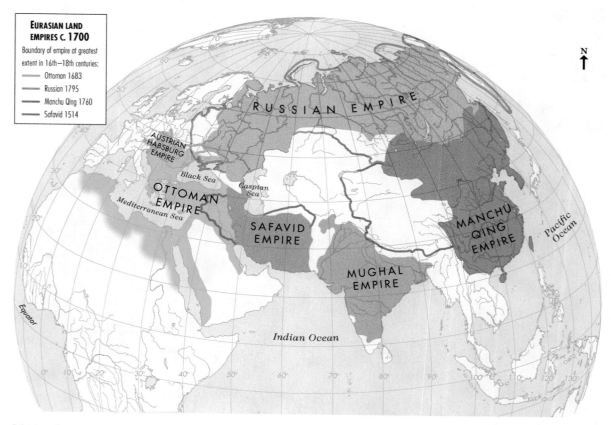

MAP 4.8 **Eurasian Land Empires, ca.1700.** The 17th and 18th centuries in Eurasia can be seen as a second "Age of Empires". Note that the success of these empires finally closed off and neutralized the nomadic pastoralists of central Asia as a major force.

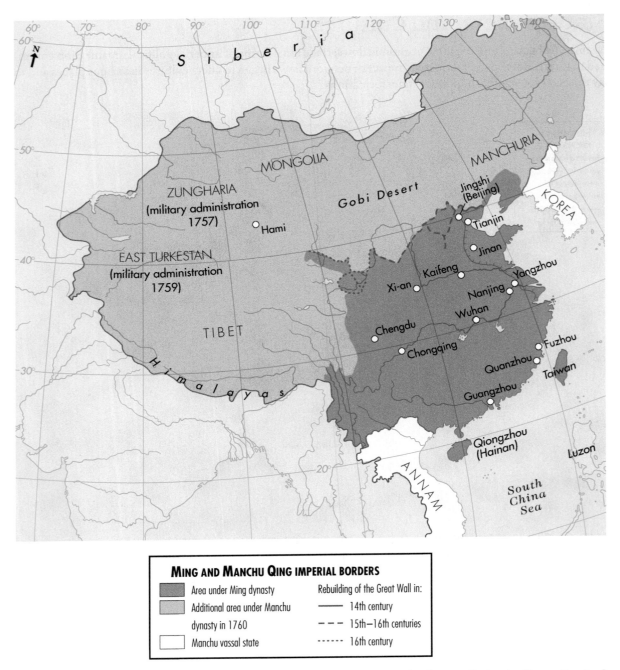

MING AND MANCHU QING IMPERIAL BORDERS

Area under Ming dynasty

Additional area under Manchu dynasty in 1760

Manchu vassal state

Rebuilding of the Great Wall in:

——— 14th century

– – – 15th–16th centuries

········· 16th century

MAP 4.9 **Ming and Manchu.** The closing of the steppes was the work of states that actually synthesized nomadic and sedentary military strengths. The semi-nomadic Manchus, who overthrew the Ming Dynasty in 1644, built such a system that allowed them to dominate vast areas of central Asia.

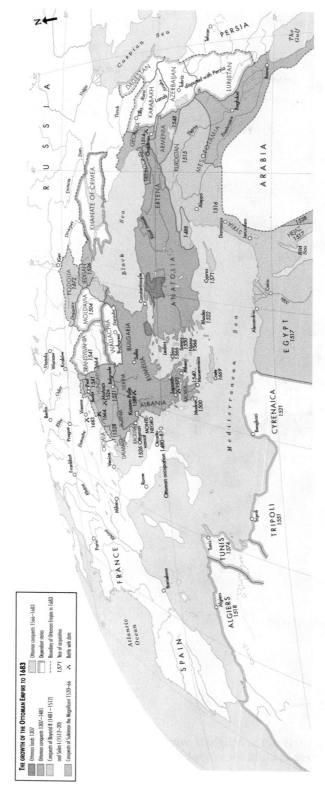

MAP 4.10 **Growth of the Ottoman Empire.** The Ottoman Turks, whose origins were nomadic but who ruled a rich sedentary empire, also used the complementary strengths of nomadic cavalry and sedentary infantry armed with muskets and cannon to build a successful empire.

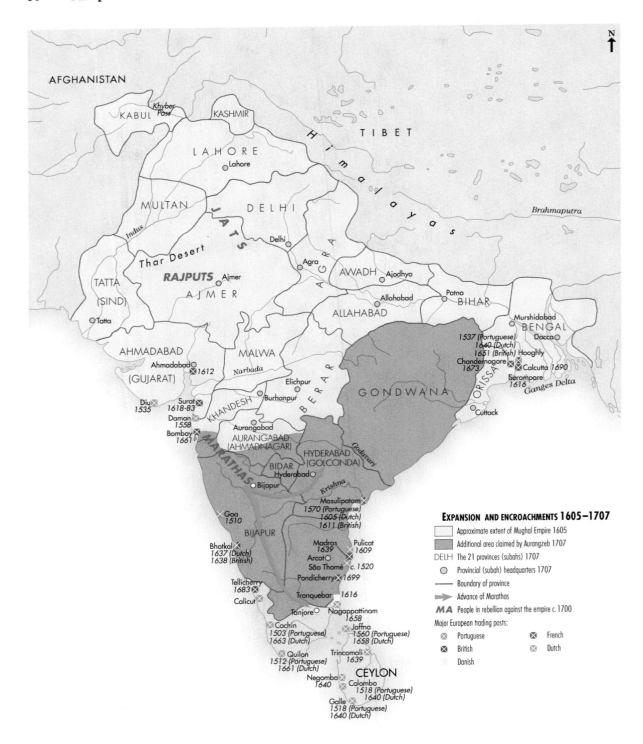

MAP 4.11 Mughal Expansion. The Mughals, whose origins lay on the steppes like the Ottomans', used the same sort of military system to build the largest sub-continental empire since the Mauryas.

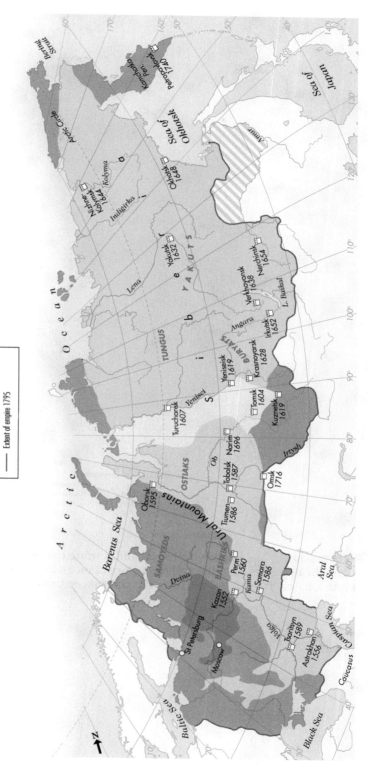

THE GROWTH OF THE RUSSIAN EMPIRE

- Russian territory 1462
- Acquisitions 1462–1533
- Acquisitions 1533–98
- Acquisitions 1598–1619
- Acquisitions 1619–89
- Occupied by Russia 1644–89
- Acquisitions 1689–1795
- Main trading post/fortress (ostrog), with date of foundation
- **OST** Native people
- Extent of empire 1795

MAP 4.12 **Russian Expansion.** The Russian Empire, too, expanded by combining Cossack steppe cavalry with drilled infantry. But Russian merchants and settlers also moved into the fur-trading regions of Siberia, subjugating native hunter-gatherers and in effect colonizing the network itself.

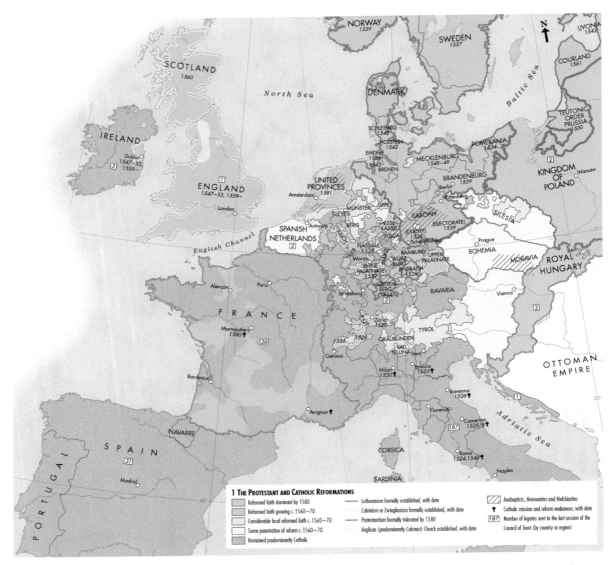

MAP 4.13 **Reformations.** The religious upheaval and warfare that accompanied the Protestant Reformation and the Catholic responses to it, the Catholic Reformation and the Counter-Reformation, illustrate the cultural encounters, both intra-cultural and inter-cultural, that occurred in a more globally networked world.

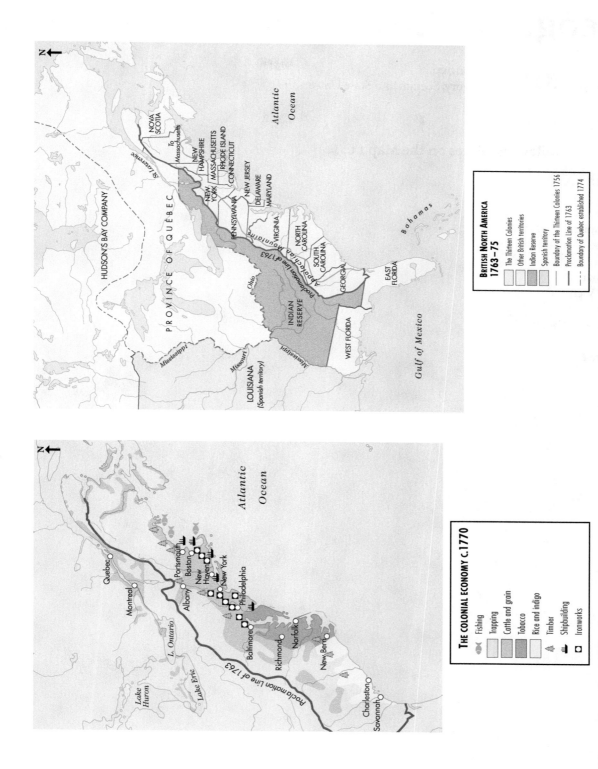

MAP 4.14 **American Colonies.** It was in British North America that globally-connected economic development and the peculiar structures of English political organization combined by 1776 to produce revolutionary political results. Even more fundamental revolutions would soon follow.

Geography Exercises

Prepared by Candace R. Gregory, Sacramento State University

Chapter 1

Label the following places on the Map 1.1:

Hadar
Kenya
Ethiopia
Ethiopian Highlands
Sahara
Sahel
Kalahari
Lake Victoria
Lake Nyssa
Great Rift Valley
Blue Nile
White Nile

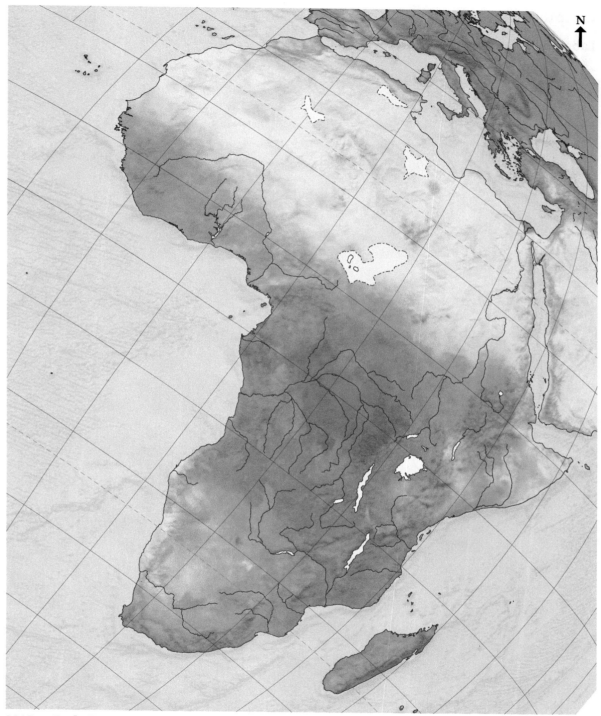

MAP 1.1 **Early Human Origins to 3 Million Years Ago**

Chapter 2

Label the following places on the Map 2.2:

Tigris River
Euphrates River
TepeGawra
Eshnunna
Tell Agrab
Uruk
Eridu
Ur
Mari
Nile River
Sinai
Mediterranean Sea
Anatolia
Persian Gulf
Zagros Mountains

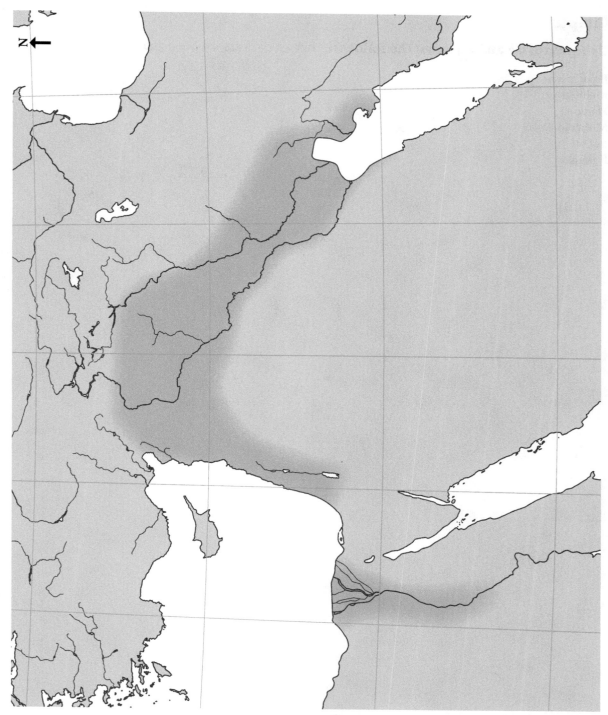

MAP 2.2 **Urban Centers in Mesopotamia and Egypt, 5500-350 BCE**

Chapter 3

Using Maps 3.2 and 3.4, label the following urban centers on Map 3.4:

Baluchistan
Mehrgarh
Harappa
Mohenjo-Daro
Lothal
Kalinga

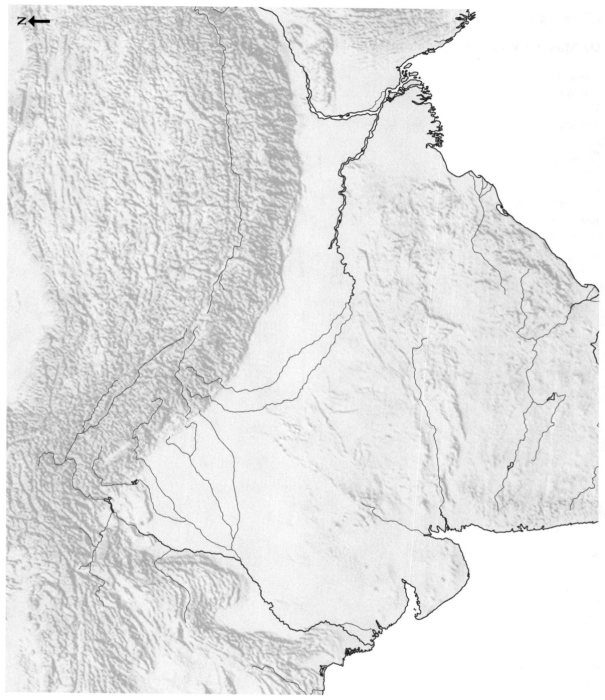

MAP 3.4 **Northern India, ca.** 650 BCE

Chapter 4

On Map 4.3, mark the trade routes and label the following cities:

Taixicun
Xingtai
Yin
Anyang
Huixian
Shang
Anyi
Erlifou
Zhengzhou
Louyang

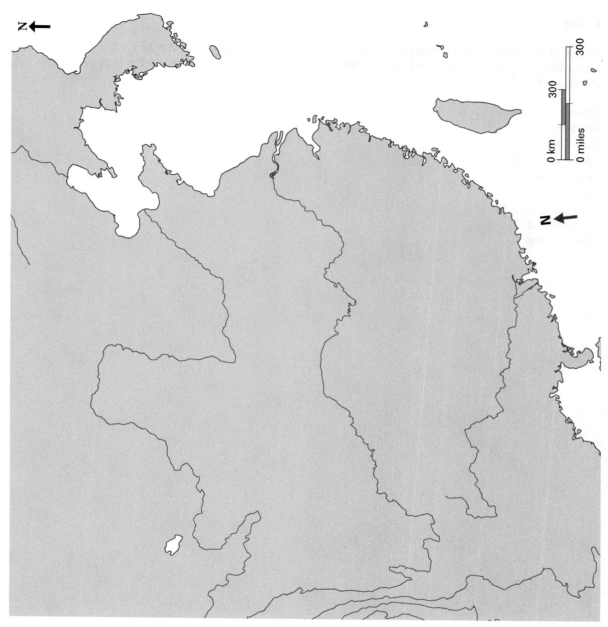

MAP 4.3 **Shang China**

Chapter 5

Trace the migration of peoples from Taiwan to New Zealand on Map 5.6, labeling the following places in order of settlement. Next to each pathway, write the possible date of migration:

Taiwan
Borneo
New Guinea
Soloman Islands
Tonga Islands
Fiji Islands
Marquesas Islands
Easter Island
New Zealand

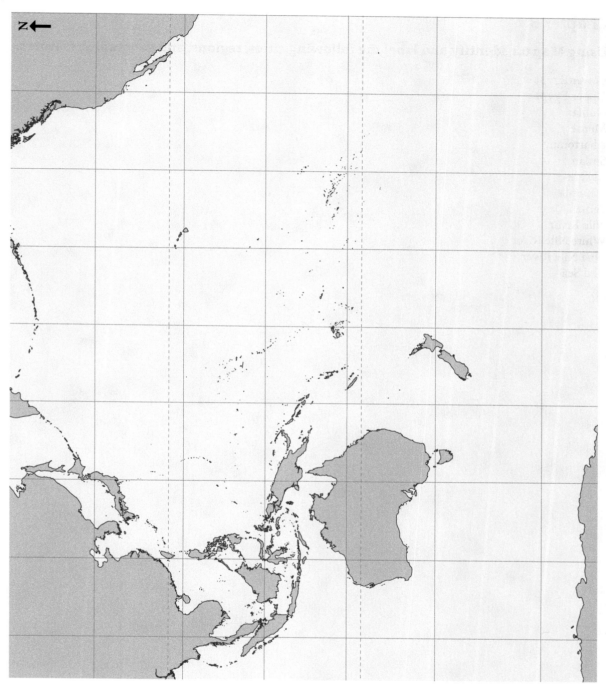

MAP 5.6 **The Colonization of the Pacific**

Chapter 6

Using Map 6.1, identify and label the following cities, regions, and geographic features:

Lower Egypt
Upper Egypt
Nubia
Meroë
Khartoum
Sudan
Aksum
Ethiopia
Yemen
Nile River
White Nile River
Blue Nile River
Red Sea

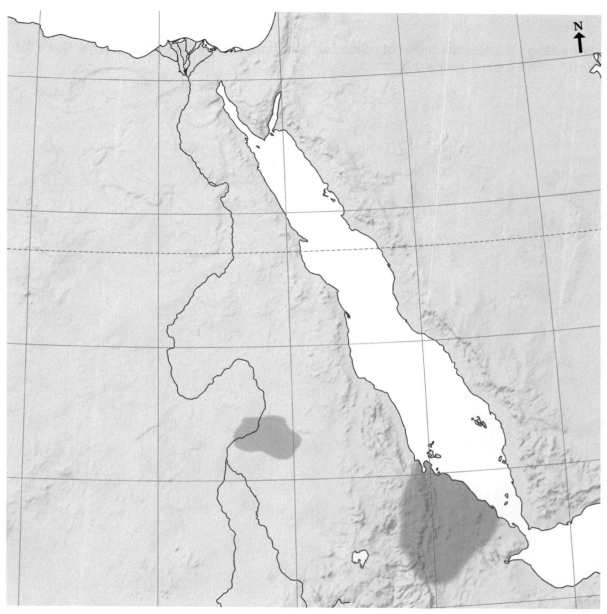

MAP 6.1 **The Kingdoms of the Meroë and Aksum, 650 BCE – 600 CE**

Chapter 7

Using Map 7.6, draw the paths of nomadic incursions for the following groups. Use a different colored pencil for each group.

Huns
Alans
Goths
Visigoths
Sarmatians
Vandals
Burgundians
Sueves
Anglo-Saxons

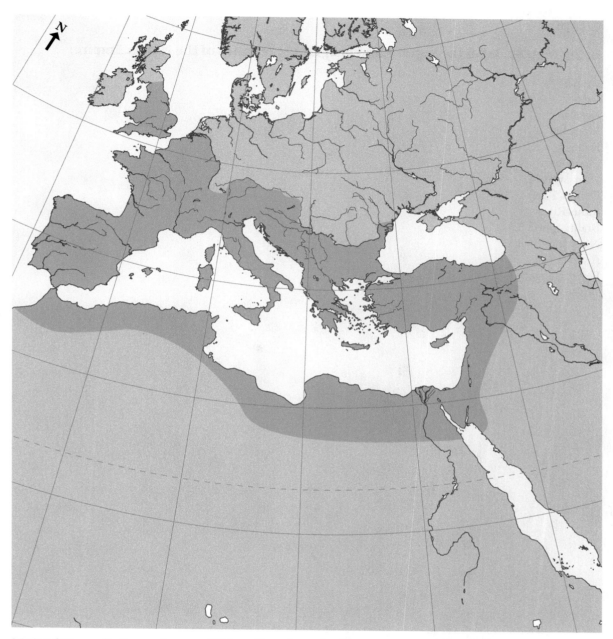

MAP 7.6 **Nomadic Incursions and Migrations into the Roman Empire, 375-450 CE**

Chapter 8

Using Map 8.1, label the regions and geographic features of the Nanda Empire:

Avanti
Vatsya
Kosala
Magadha
Kalinga
Thar Desert
Himalayas
Ganges River
Indus River
Brahmaputra River
Narmada River
Arabian Sea
Bay of Bengal

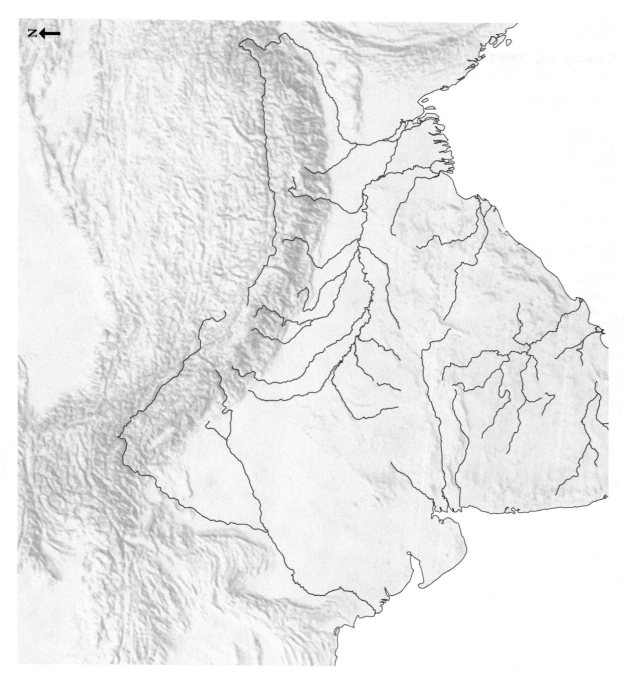

MAP 8.1 **Northern India, ca.** 400 BCE

Chapter 9

On Map 9.5, draw the routes that comprised the Silk Road. Then label the following key cities on the Silk Road:

Constantinople
Alexandria, Egypt
Antioch
Palmyra
Ctesiphon
Persepolis
Samaqara
Bukhara
Bactria
Charsala
Khotan
Kucha
Turfan
Dunhuang
Chang'an
Luoyang

MAP 9.5 **The Silk Road, ca.** 150 CE

Chapter 10

Use different colored pencils to color in the Arab conquests by the following date ranges, using Map 10.1 as a reference:

Conquests to 632
Conquests from 632 – 634
Conquests from 634 – 644
Conquests from 644 – 661
Conquests from 661 – 750

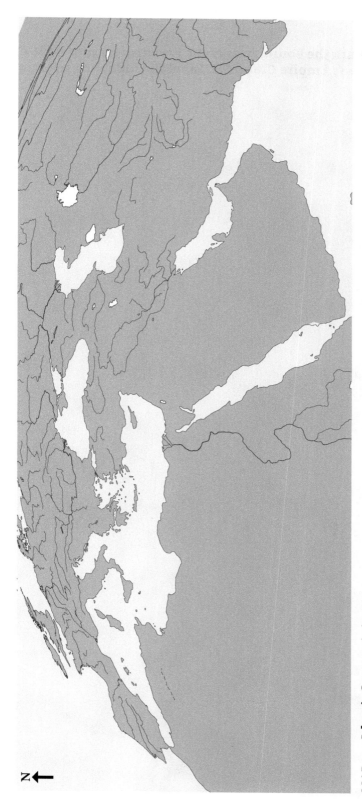

MAP 10.1 **Islamic Conquests to 750**

N

Chapter 11

Using Map 11.2, mark the boundaries of the Frankish Empire c. 768 C.E., and the boundaries of Charlemagne's Empire C. 800 C.E. Label the following urban centers:

Barcelona
Toulouse
Bordeaux
Poitiers
Tours
Orleans
Chartres
Paris
Rouen
Langres
Cologne
Verden
Worms
Speyer
Salzburg
Milan
Pavia
Florence
Rome
Monte Cassino
Benevento

N

MAP 11.2 **The Empire of Charlemagne**

Chapter 12

Using Map 12.2, label the following cities of the Eurasian Trade Routes, c. 1000 C.E.

Cairo
Alexandria
Jiddah
Mecca
Damascus
Baghdad
Antioch
Constantinople
Kaffa
Sarai
Bukhara
Samarkand
Mashhad
Heart
Shiraz
Hormuz
Dehal
Cambray
Benares
Delhi
Lahore
Peshawar
Kabul
Balkh
Kokand
Karokorum
Turfan
Dunhuang
Beijing
Luoyang
Hangzhou
Lanzhou
Quanzhou
Palembang, Vietnam
Pegu
Palembang, Sumatra
Borobdur

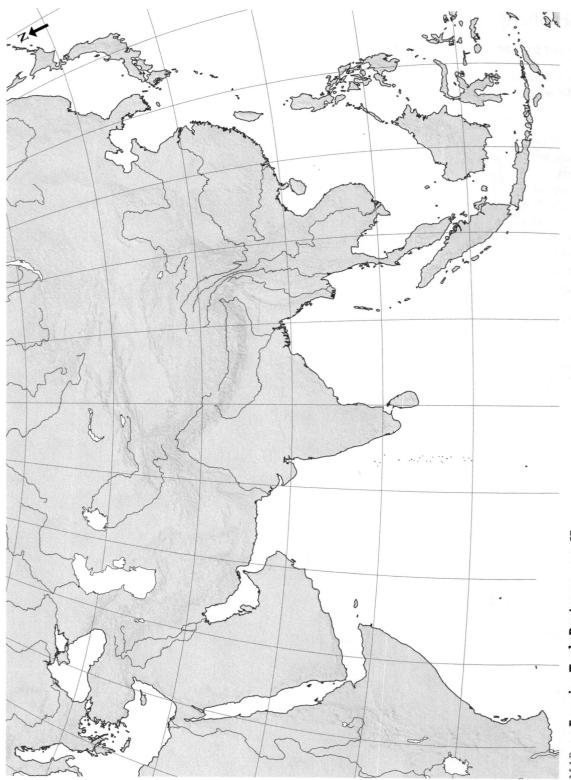

MAP 12.2 **Eurasian Trade Routes, ca.** 1000 CE

Chapter 13

Refer to Map 13.7 and label the following regions and cities in Southeast Asia:

New Guinea
Moluccas
Celebes
Mindanao
Philippines
Borneo
Java
Sumatra
Malay Peninsula
Cambodia
Vietnam
Siam
Burma
China
Hanoi
HaiPhong
Rangoon
Bangkok
Manila
Singapore
Djakarta

MAP 13.7 **Southeast Asia: The Physical Setting**

Chapter 14

On Map 14.3, label the following cities. For each city, identify one of the following trade items that was likely to have passed through its markets.

Cities:
Mogadishu
Gede
Malindi
Zanzibar
Kilwa
Sofala
Great Zimbabwe
Cambay
Calicut
Aden

Trade Items:
Gold
Ivory
Slaves
Copper
Beads
Textiles
Sugar
Glass

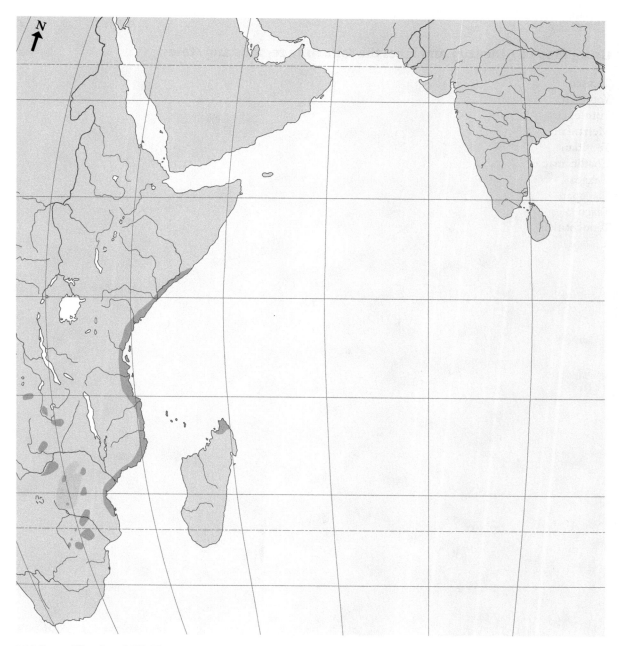

MAP 14.3 **The Swahili City-States, ca.** 1400

Chapter 15

Using Map 15.3, identify and label the following regions and states.

Tarasco
Yopitzinco
Tototepec
Metztitlan
Teotitlan
Coatlicamac
Oaxaca
Tlacopan
Texcoco
Tenochtitlán

MAP 15.3 **The Aztec Empire, ca.** 1520

Chapter 16

Using Map 16.2, and different color pencils, draw in the Ottoman conquests and expansions to the empire for the following dates.

1307 lands
1307 – 1481
1481 – 1520
1520 – 1566
1566 – 1683

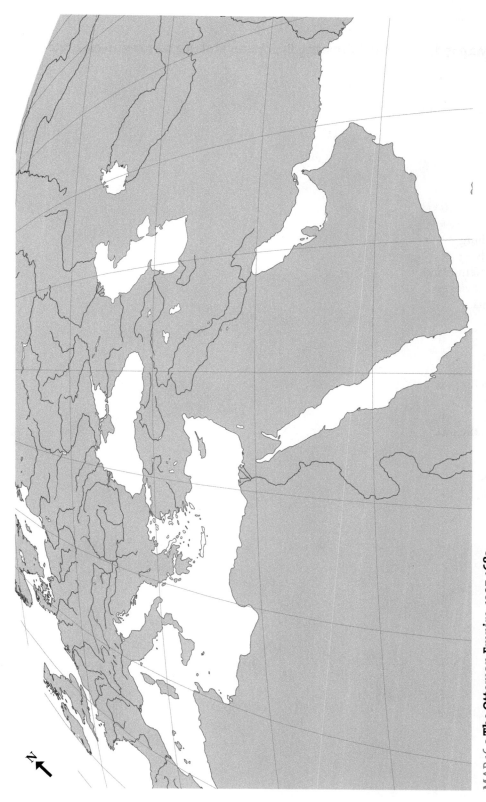

MAP 16.3 **The Ottoman Empire, 1307-1683**

Chapter 17

Using Map 17.2, label the following European states and provinces, c. 1580.

Portugal
Spain
Navarre
France
Alsace
Savoy
Austria
Bavaria
Saxony
Brandenburg
Mecklenburg
Spanish Netherlands
United Provinces
Pomerania
England
Ireland
Scotland
Italy
Ottoman Empire
Hungary
Bohemia
Poland-Lithuania
Russia
Norway
Sweden
Finland

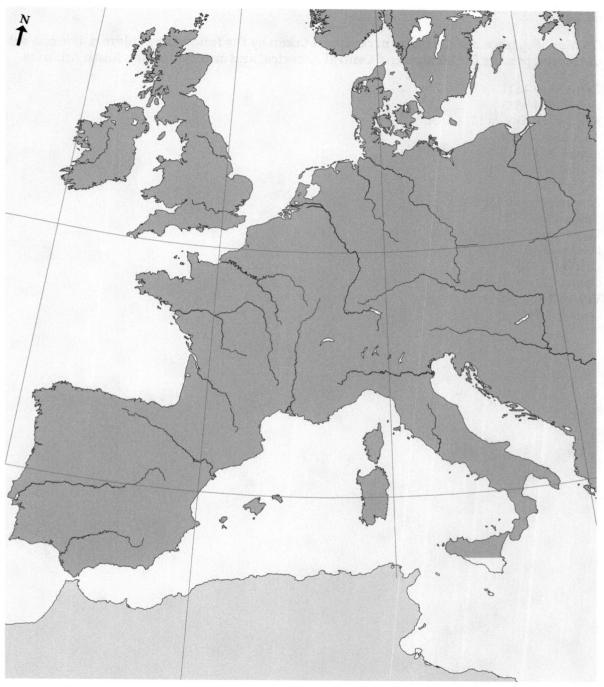

MAP 17.2 **The Protestant Reformation, ca.** 1580

Chapter 18

On Map 18.1, trace out the paths of conquest taken by the following explorers. Use one set of colored pencils for Mexico and Central America, and another set for South America.

Cortés 1519-1521
Cortés 1524-1525
Narváez and da Vaca 1528-1536
De Soto 1539-1545
Alarcon 1540
Coronado 1540-1542
Cabot 1526
Francisco Pizarro 1531-1533
Amalgro 1535-1537
Federmann 1537-1539
Benalcazar 1538-1539
Orrellana 1540
Gonzalo Pizarro 1540-1542
Valdivia 1540-1547
Quesada 1542

MAP 18.1 **The European Exploration of the Americas, 1519-1542**

Concept Maps and Exercises

Exercises prepared by Robert Bond, San Diego Mesa Community College.

Chapter 1

1. How is the idea of "deep time" expressed in the Concept Map?
2. Does the Concept Map demonstrate the incredibly short amount of time H. sapiens has inhabited the earth?
3. How does this awareness affect the way you think about human history?

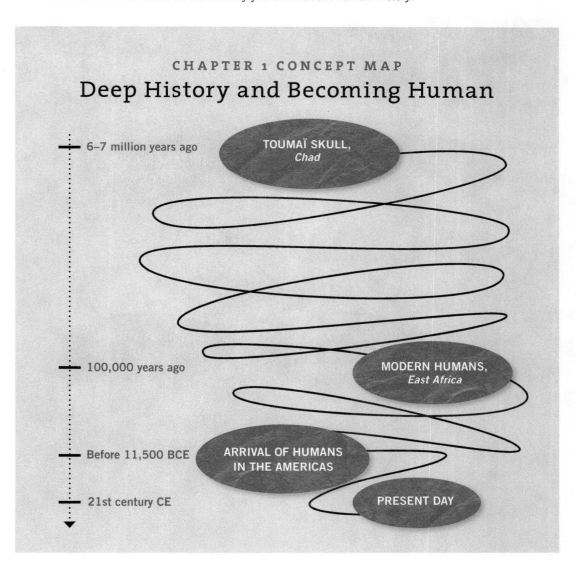

CHAPTER 1 CONCEPT MAP

Deep History and Becoming Human

6–7 million years ago — TOUMAÏ SKULL, *Chad*

100,000 years ago — MODERN HUMANS, *East Africa*

Before 11,500 BCE — ARRIVAL OF HUMANS IN THE AMERICAS

21st century CE — PRESENT DAY

Chapter 2

1. How are the patterns behind the creation of agrarian-urban society displayed in the Concept Map?
2. Does the Concept Map point to the often harsh inequalities that accompanied early agrarian-urban societies?

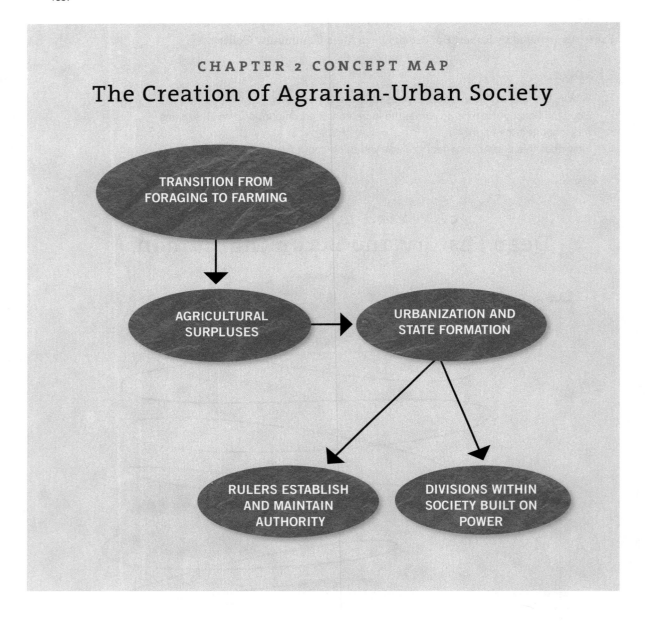

CHAPTER 2 CONCEPT MAP

The Creation of Agrarian-Urban Society

TRANSITION FROM FORAGING TO FARMING

AGRICULTURAL SURPLUSES

URBANIZATION AND STATE FORMATION

RULERS ESTABLISH AND MAINTAIN AUTHORITY

DIVISIONS WITHIN SOCIETY BUILT ON POWER

CHAPTER 3

1. Discuss and give an example of the traditional (customary) view of history as being linear.
2. Discuss and give an example of the non-traditional (non-customary) view of history as being a continual process of interaction and adaptation.
3. Which view of history does Harappan civilization relate to? Why?
4. Review the Aryan settlement of India. What view of history do you think it represents?
5. Using the diagram "Non-Customary View" as a guide, show the various stages of Harappan development and eventual decline. What are some of the factors (interactions and adaptations) which led to each stage?
6. Are there other ways that historians could view the progress of history?

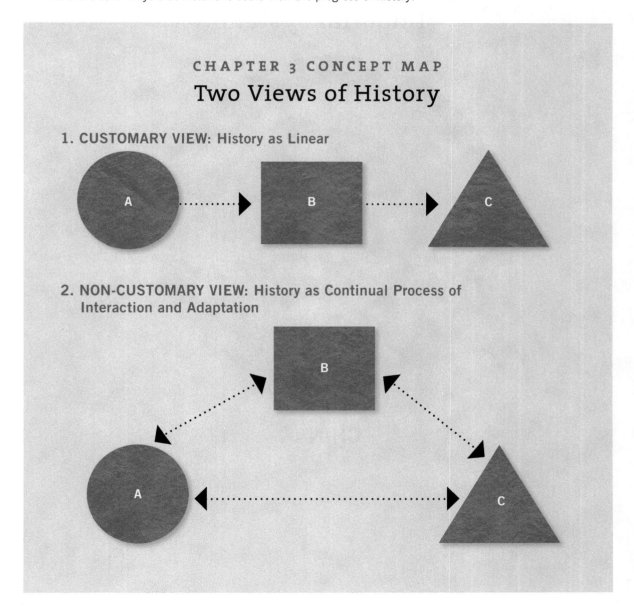

Chapter 4

1. How does the Concept Map show centrality of the emperor in the Chinese imperial system?
2. Why is China's writing system a source of power?

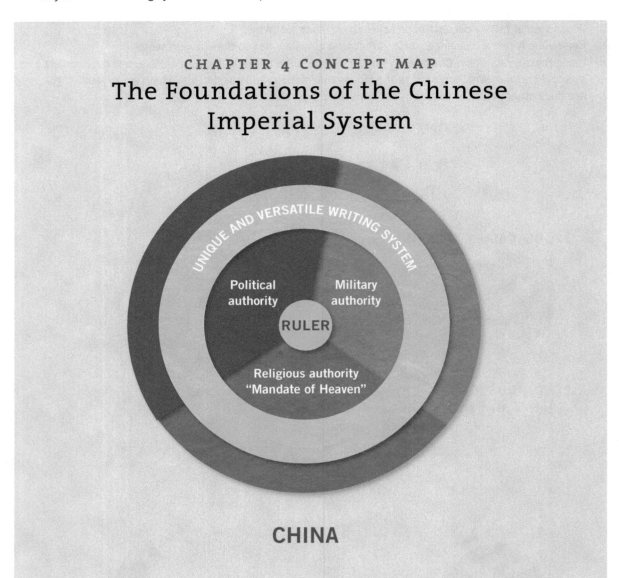

CHAPTER 4 CONCEPT MAP

The Foundations of the Chinese Imperial System

UNIQUE AND VERSATILE WRITING SYSTEM

Political authority

Military authority

RULER

Religious authority
"Mandate of Heaven"

CHINA

Chapter 5

1. How does this Concept Map show common patterns across widely separated cultures of the world?
2. Does an appreciation for foundational patterns across widely divergent societies alter the way you think about the Americas and Oceania in this period in world history?

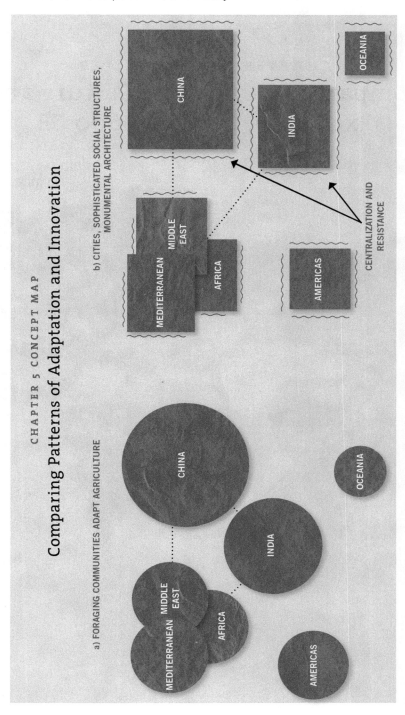

CHAPTER 5 CONCEPT MAP

Comparing Patterns of Adaptation and Innovation

a) FORAGING COMMUNITIES ADAPT AGRICULTURE

b) CITIES, SOPHISTICATED SOCIAL STRUCTURES, MONUMENTAL ARCHITECTURE

CENTRALIZATION AND RESISTANCE

CHINA · INDIA · OCEANIA · MEDITERRANEAN · MIDDLE EAST · AFRICA · AMERICAS

Chapter 6

1. How does this Concept Map show the expanding networks of trade and communication in the period 600 BCE – 600 CE?
2. Do Sub-Saharan Africa and the Americas display the same patterns as Eurasia and North Africa?

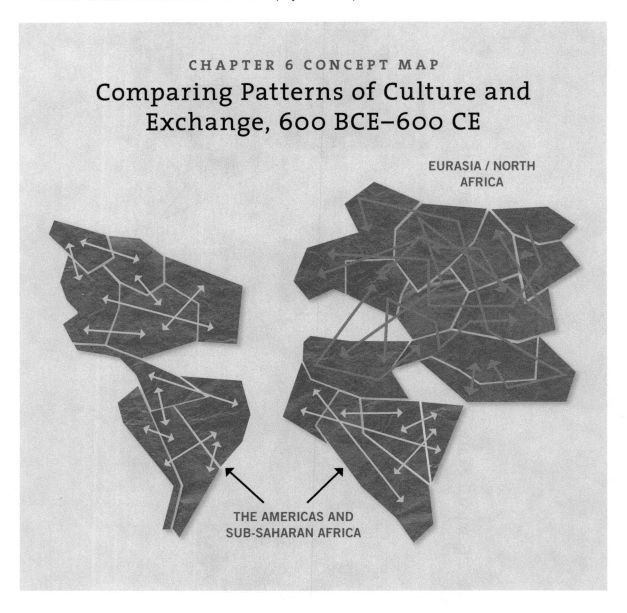

CHAPTER 6 CONCEPT MAP
Comparing Patterns of Culture and Exchange, 600 BCE–600 CE

EURASIA / NORTH AFRICA

THE AMERICAS AND SUB-SAHARAN AFRICA

Chapter 7

1. Why do(es) God/ the gods interact with the Empire/Earth?
2. Why does God not interact with the Commonwealth of Multiple Kingdoms?
3. As indicated by the arrows, how does the Commonwealth of Multiple Kingdoms interact with one another? How is this different from the interaction found in polytheism?

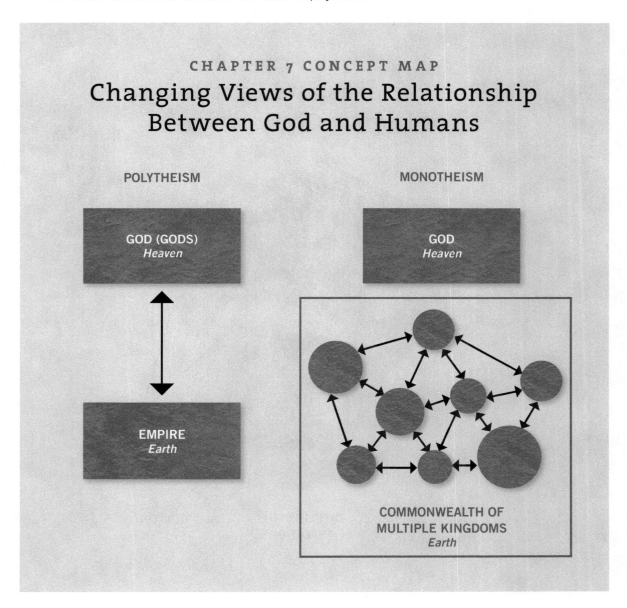

Chapter 8

1. Why was there so much political disunity in India?
2. With no political unity, what holds India together?
3. Give some examples of India's religious, intellectual and cultural traditions. How are these various religious, intellectual and cultural traditions related to one other?

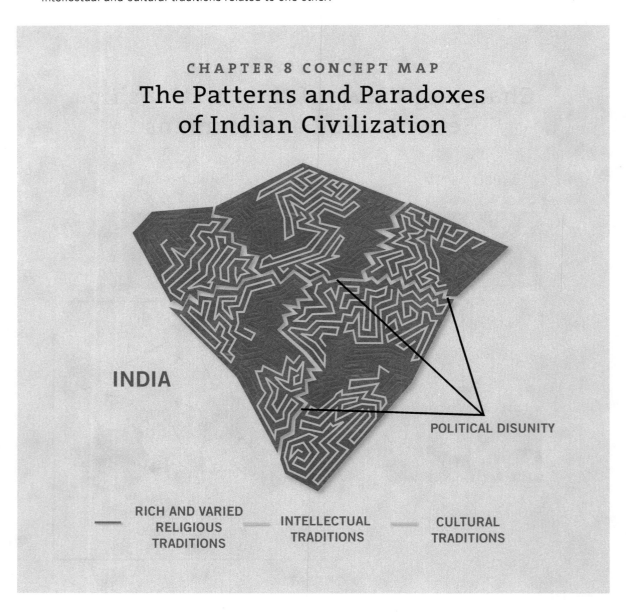

CHAPTER 8 CONCEPT MAP

The Patterns and Paradoxes of Indian Civilization

INDIA

POLITICAL DISUNITY

RICH AND VARIED RELIGIOUS TRADITIONS — INTELLECTUAL TRADITIONS — CULTURAL TRADITIONS

Chapter 9

1. Why is "Social Harmony" so important to "Politics" and "Society?"
2. What is "the Way?"
3. What concrete applications did Chinese philosophers come up with for social and political harmony? What is the role of the emperor in this system? Bureaucrats?
4. Analyze Confucianism, Legalism and Daoism using the map as a model. Why is the group and collective action more important than the individual in social and political affairs? How does this compare to ancient Greek civilization? Did Shi Huangdi act in accordance with the traditional Chinese view of society and order?

CHAPTER 9 CONCEPT MAP

Traditional Chinese View of Human Society and the Cosmos

	POLITICS	SOCIETY	PHILOSOPHY
BASIC UNIT	Empire	The group	Relationship of the part to the whole
GOAL	Social harmony	Social harmony	The Way (*Dao*)
METHODS	Collective action (Legalism)	Obligations to family and society (Confucianism)	Search for concrete applications

Chapter 10

1. How did Greek philosophy influence early Christianity and Islam?
2. What influence did Judaic monotheism have on the development of early Christianity and Islam?
3. What is the difference between early Christianity and Eastern Christianity? What can we conclude about the various cultural elements which influenced Eastern Christianity and Islam?

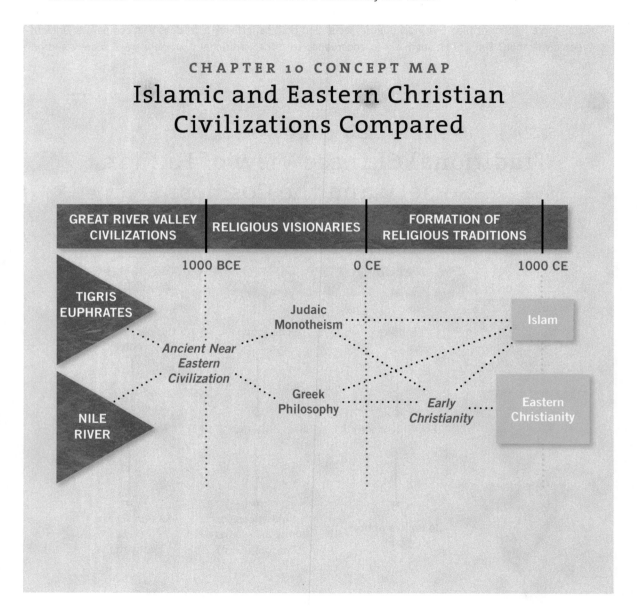

CHAPTER 10 CONCEPT MAP

Islamic and Eastern Christian Civilizations Compared

Chapter 11

1. Give specific examples of how each of the elements making up Latin Christendom contributed to this synthesis.
2. Based on the map, how did European civilization innovate? adapt?
3. Have we encountered other examples of similar processes of synthesis happening elsewhere in the world at this time?

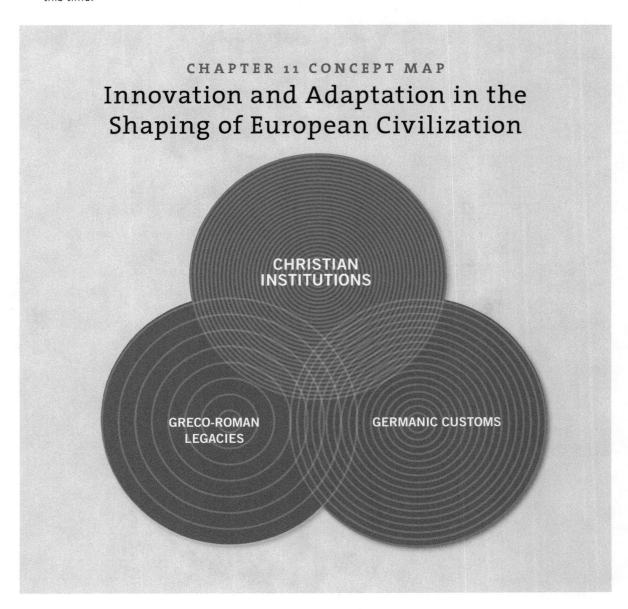

CHAPTER 11 CONCEPT MAP

Innovation and Adaptation in the Shaping of European Civilization

CHRISTIAN INSTITUTIONS

GRECO-ROMAN LEGACIES

GERMANIC CUSTOMS

Chapter 12

1. How does this map show the differences between "syncretism" and "synthesis?"
2. How did Confucianism, Daoism and Buddhism each contribute to the development of Neo-Confucianism in China?
3. Why did China's religious synthesis serve as a unifying force? How did India experience a different pattern?

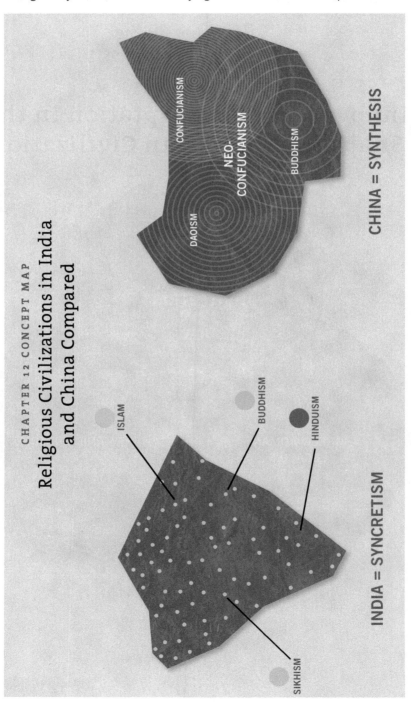

CHAPTER 12 CONCEPT MAP

Religious Civilizations in India and China Compared

CHINA = SYNTHESIS

INDIA = SYNCRETISM

Chapter 13

1. In what ways did China influence its neighbors?
2. How did Japan, Korea, and Vietnam adapt Chinese culture in their own unique ways?
3. How did each use Chinese culture as a force for state-building?

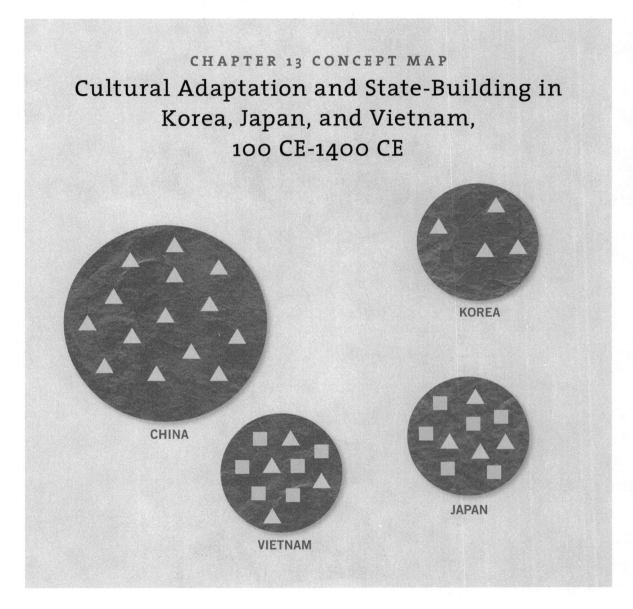

CHAPTER 13 CONCEPT MAP

Cultural Adaptation and State-Building in Korea, Japan, and Vietnam, 100 CE-1400 CE

Chapter 14

1. How is "top-down" history different from "bottom-up" history?
2. What are the advantages and disadvantages of each approach to African history?
3. Are there any other areas in the world which might benefit from a "bottom-up" approach to history?

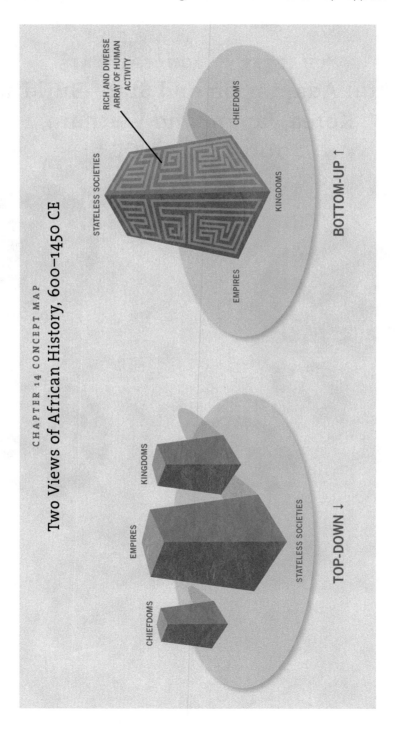

CHAPTER 14 CONCEPT MAP

Two Views of African History, 600–1450 CE

RICH AND DIVERSE ARRAY OF HUMAN ACTIVITY

STATELESS SOCIETIES

CHIEFDOMS

KINGDOMS

EMPIRES

BOTTOM-UP ↑

KINGDOMS

EMPIRES

STATELESS SOCIETIES

CHIEFDOMS

TOP-DOWN ↓

Chapter 15

1. How can we explain similarities in patterns of development in both the Americas and Eurasia?
2. What types of regional variations were there? Give examples.
3. How do these patterns compare when viewed on a timeline?
4. Using examples, compare the development of intensive agriculture, military states and empires, and temple-based city states in both the Americas and Eurasia.

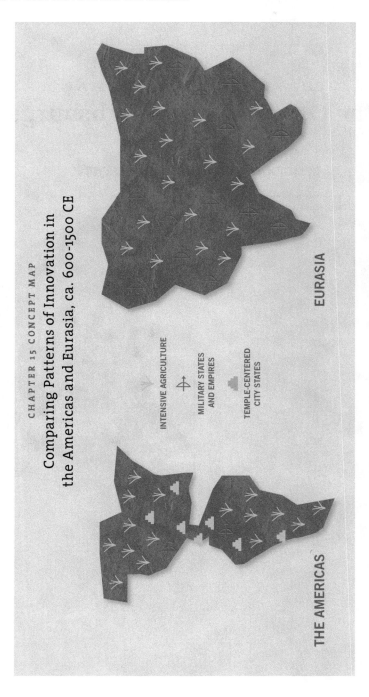

CHAPTER 15 CONCEPT MAP

Comparing Patterns of Innovation in the Americas and Eurasia, ca. 600–1500 CE

INTENSIVE AGRICULTURE

MILITARY STATES AND EMPIRES

TEMPLE-CENTERED CITY STATES

EURASIA

THE AMERICAS

Chapter 16

1. What is a "fiscal-military" state? Does the Ottoman and Habsburg Empires both fit into that definition? Why?

2. What is "imperialism"? Were both empires "imperialistic"? Why?

3. In what ways did these empires project their power and grandeur?

4. Does this Concept Map change the way you think about the interactions between the Ottomans and the Habsburgs?

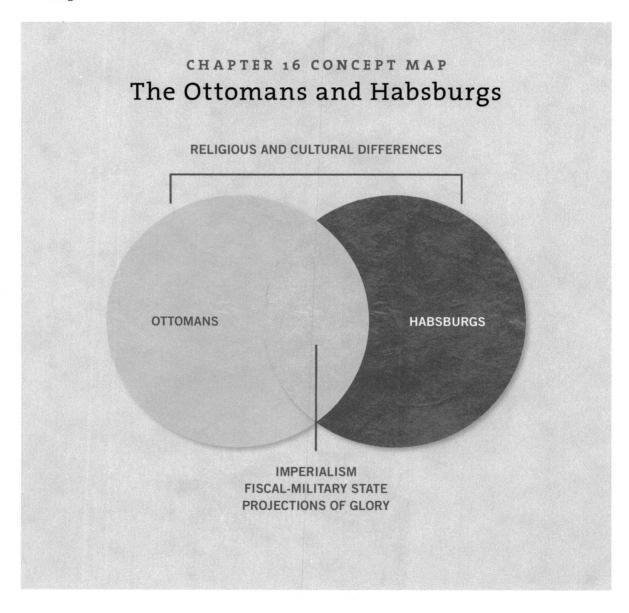

CHAPTER 16 CONCEPT MAP
The Ottomans and Habsburgs

RELIGIOUS AND CULTURAL DIFFERENCES

OTTOMANS   HABSBURGS

IMPERIALISM
FISCAL-MILITARY STATE
PROJECTIONS OF GLORY

Chapter 17

1. Examine the Concept Map closely. Why is each stage important to the development of the next stage?
2. Why is the mathematization of astronomy and physics perhaps the most important development?
3. What would have been the outcome if descriptive science had never been rendered obsolete?

CHAPTER 17 CONCEPT MAP

The Development of the New Science in the West

Greece, Rome, Islamic science, and medieval Christianity

Since 1500

1700

1800

Descriptive Science (Aristotle)

Mathematization of astronomy and physics

Application of science to industry

Industrialization

Chapter 18

1. What is the major change that in the relationship between Europe and India and China that occurs between 1500 and 1800?
2. What does the change in the relative sizes of each region indicate? Why advantages did the American tropics and subtropics confer on Europe?
3. How does this Concept Map show the importance of the environment in world history?

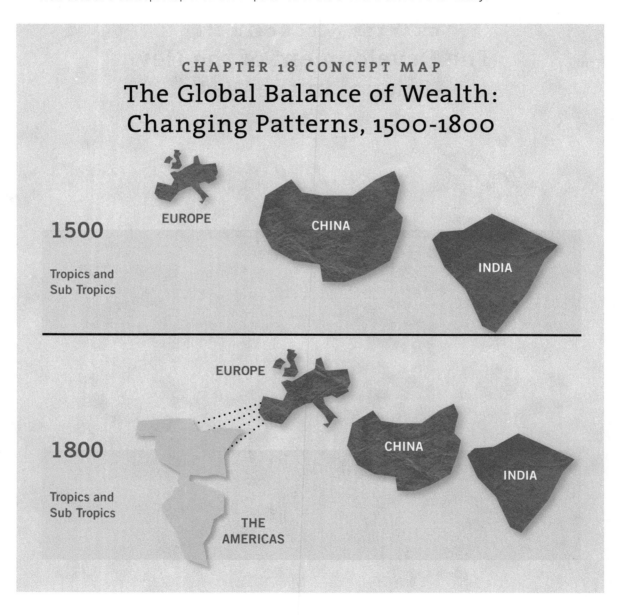

CHAPTER 18 CONCEPT MAP
The Global Balance of Wealth: Changing Patterns, 1500-1800

Chapter 19

1. Examine the two ways of looking at the Atlantic World in this period.   What is revealed when one focuses on trade?   What dynamics are evident when looks at social and cultural patterns?
2. Can one fully appreciate African, European, and American history in this period without including both perspectives?

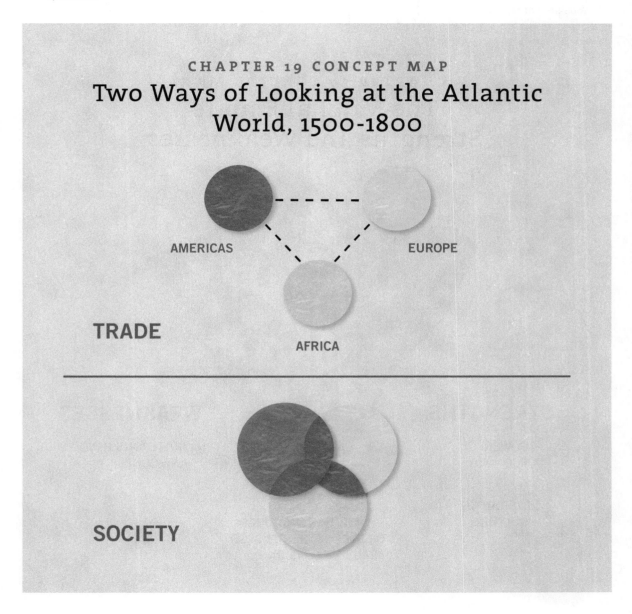

CHAPTER 19 CONCEPT MAP

Two Ways of Looking at the Atlantic World, 1500-1800

AMERICAS

EUROPE

AFRICA

TRADE

SOCIETY

Chapter 20

1. What were the sources of the strength of the Mughal economy? What role did geography play?
2. How did the Mughals contribute to Indian culture?
3. What syncretic religions emerged in India during the Mughal period? Why did they emerge?
4. What were the roots of conflict in the Mughal Empire? Were they only caused by religious differences between Muslim and Hindu?

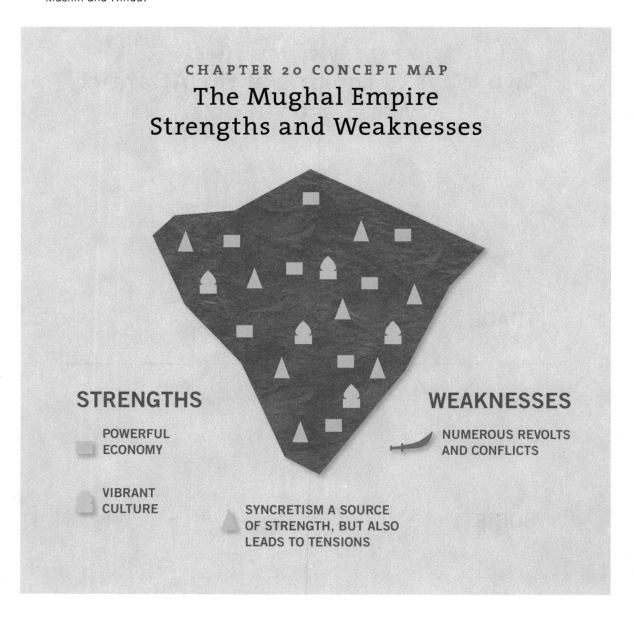

CHAPTER 20 CONCEPT MAP
The Mughal Empire
Strengths and Weaknesses

STRENGTHS

POWERFUL
ECONOMY

VIBRANT
CULTURE

SYNCRETISM A SOURCE
OF STRENGTH, BUT ALSO
LEADS TO TENSIONS

WEAKNESSES

NUMEROUS REVOLTS
AND CONFLICTS

Chapter 21

1. Does the Concept Map reveal the differences in the "inner domains" of China and Japan?
2. Does the Concept Map reveal the different ways Japan and China controlled their "inner domains"?
3. How does the Concept Map show the different ways Japan and China regarded their "outer domains"?

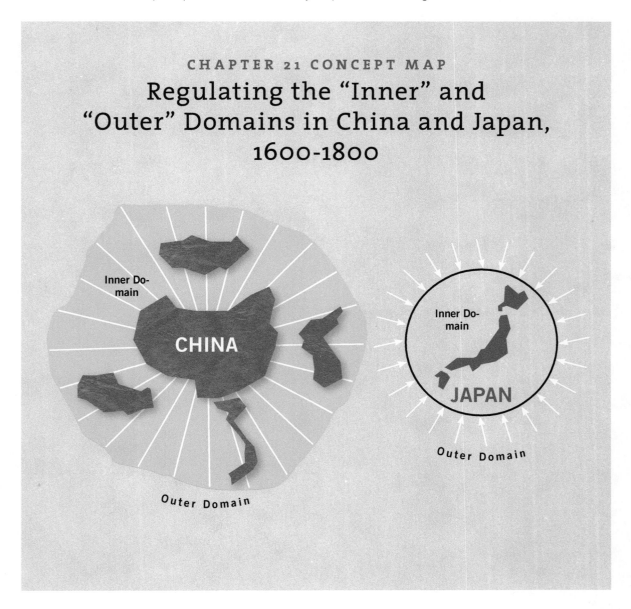

CHAPTER 21 CONCEPT MAP
Regulating the "Inner" and "Outer" Domains in China and Japan, 1600-1800

NOTES

NOTES

Index